# Pillsbury Bake-Off® winners

100 Top Recipes from the
42nd Pillsbury Bake-Off® Contest

BICENTENNIAL
1807
WILEY
2007
BICENTENNIAL

Wiley Publishing, Inc.

Published by Wiley Publishing, Inc., Hoboken, NJ

For general information on our other products and services or to obtain technical support please contact our Customer Care Department within the U.S. at 800-762-2974, outside the U.S. at 317-572-3993 or fax 317-572-4002.

Wiley also publishes its books in a variety of electronic formats. Some content that appears in print may not be available in electronic books. For more information about Wiley products, visit our web site at www.wiley.com.

**LIBRARY OF CONGRESS CATALOGING-IN-PUBLICATION DATA:**

Pillsbury bake-off winners : 100 top recipes from the 42nd Pillsbury bake-off contest / Pillsbury editors.

    p. cm.

Includes index.

ISBN: 978-0-470-08061-0 (cloth)

1. Baking. 2. Cookery, American. I. C.A. Pillsbury and Company.

TX765.P51927 2007

641.8'15--dc22

        2006032484

Manufactured in the United States of America

10 9 8 7 6 5 4 3 2

Cover photo: Peanut Butter Truffle Tart (page 188)

## GENERAL MILLS

Publisher, Books and Magazines:
**Sheila Burke**

Manager, Cookbook Publishing:
**Lois Tlusty**

Editor: **Sharon Secor**

Food Editor: **Lola Whalen**

Recipe Development and Testing:
**Pillsbury Kitchens**

Photography: **General Mills Photography Studios and Image Library**

Photographer: **Val Bourassa**

Food Stylists: **Carol Grones; Cindy Syme**

## WILEY PUBLISHING, INC.

Publisher: **Natalie Chapman**

Executive Editor: **Anne Ficklen**

Editorial Assistant: **Charleen Barila**

Editor: **Kristi Hart**

Production Editor: **Amy Zarkos**

Cover Design: **Suzanne Sunwoo**

Art Director: **Tai Blanche**

Manufacturing Manager: **Kevin Watt**

Wiley Bicentennial Logo:
**Richard J. Pacifico**

Home of the Pillsbury Bake-Off® Contest

Pillsbury

Our recipes have been tested in the Pillsbury Kitchens and meet our standards of easy preparation, reliability and great taste.

For more great recipes visit pillsbury.com

## Dear Friends,

There's nothing more exciting than the Pillsbury Bake-Off® Contest! At least that's the way 100 finalists felt as they stepped up to their ranges to begin cooking for America's premier cooking competition, the 42nd Pillsbury Bake-Off® Contest in Orlando, Florida, on March 21, 2006.

The contest originated in 1949, with the first competition at the Waldorf-Astoria Hotel in New York City. The contest was held annually from 1949 to 1978, when it switched to an every-other-year schedule. The $1 million Grand Prize was first awarded in 1996 to Kurt Wait, who was also the first man to win top honors in the contest.

Each of the 100 recipes chosen by the Pillsbury Bake-Off® Kitchens for inclusion in the contest—and in this book—are from among thousands of recipes submitted. Every single one of the recipes is someone's special creation, an everyday connection to home, family and friends. Each recipe also provides a sneak peek into what's happening in kitchens around the country and what foods and flavors are gaining popularity on America's kitchen tables.

In the end, only one recipe can win the Grand Prize in the Pillsbury Bake-Off® Contest but 99 other cooks go home knowing that their recipe creations are among America's best. And we, having sampled them all, certainly agree!

We've collected them all here for you to enjoy—100 great recipes from home cooks across the country to make, savor and enjoy with your family.

Sincerely,

*Lola Whalen*

Lola Whalen
Kitchen Manager,
42nd Pillsbury
Bake-Off® Contest

# contents

# memories and recipes of the pillsbury bake-off® contest

**There's a story behind every recipe.** What makes a memory? Grandma's rhubarb pie or Aunt Rafina's family favorite—a curry sauce she makes every Thanksgiving. Food is a link to our family and friends. It becomes part of our family history and memories. "Remember when Dad made . . ." sets the stage for family stories.

fun fact: The first contest was held in 1949 at New York City's Waldorf-Astoria Hotel. Electricity from nearby subway tracks was needed to power the finalists' 100 new General Electric Stratoliner ranges because the Grand Ballroom lacked alternating current.

**Bake-Off® recipes are family stories too.** Every one of the 100 recipes in this book was created by an ordinary woman or man who wanted to create a special moment and memory for family and friends. You'll be introduced to them all and learn why each contestant created their dish. (Hint—it wasn't to win a million dollars!)

**Add your memories to the Bake-Off® family album.** To create your own special moments, enjoy the homemade goodness of these winning recipes. They reflect the tastes and trends of American homes just like yours. Pick your favorites to make again and again for family and friends.

## the first bake-off® contest

The first Pillsbury Bake-Off® Contest in 1949 spurred a phenomenon that many copied but few have perfected over the years. Throughout the 1950s, the contest showcased the creativity of America's best home cooks and their favorite new flavors in the kitchen.

The very first contestants

## times have changed

These days, the 100 Bake-Off® recipes represent every culture of the American landscape. Food trends are widespread: Mexican-inspired flavors and lower-calorie cooking today are as popular as desserts and casseroles were in the 1950s. Entries in recent contests reflect a passion for flavor and an increase in nutrition knowledge among amateur cooks.

## setting up for the big day

Before finalists arrive at the contest, the Bake-Off® team is hard at work. Six semi-trucks filled with cabinets, refrigerators, ranges, microwave ovens and equipment arrive three days before the contest. Floor assistants set up 100 mini-kitchens for the event and stock each kitchen on the contest floor. Each one has all the cooking and baking supplies the finalist needs to make their unique recipe.

## the 42nd bake-off® contest

Finalists from 35 different states gather in Orlando, Florida, on the edge of the official contest floor, ready to compete for the dough—the $1 million Grand Prize.

fun fact: Each of the 100 finalists, who are chosen from among tens of thousands of entries, wins a three-night stay at a fabulous hotel and spending money.

fun fact: The kitchen equipment list for the finalists includes: 437 mixing bowls, 309 rubber spatulas, 238 wooden spoons, 172 measuring spoon sets, 168 measuring cup sets, 147 glass measuring cups, 117 cookie sheets, 90 skillets and 89 cookie racks.

fun fact:
- Three finalists are men.
- Finalists range in age from 20 to 67.
- California has the most finalists with 12. Texas follows next with seven.
- Finalist's careers range from pre-school teacher to computer consultant, college professor to financial controller. Twenty-one finalists are stay-at-home moms.

fun fact: The Pillsburys have attended nearly every Bake-Off® Contest since it began in 1949, and they visited this year's finalists at their mini-kitchens.

fun fact: Some contestants say that if they win the contest, they will:

- Attend cooking schools in China and France.
- Build a chocolate factory.
- Start a cooking program at an elementary school.
- Open a kitchen or cookbook store.
- Travel around the world to experience and learn about food from other countries.

fun fact: While finalists are preparing their dishes, one Pillsbury employee waits at a local supermarket with a phone, just in case a missing ingredient is needed.

fun fact: One finalist wasn't able to participate. She had a good reason. She was expecting the birth of a baby—born, in fact, the day after the contest. Actually, several previous contests have been conducted with 99 finalists too. The most common reason for finalist absence? Awaiting a baby's birth.

# cooking for the $1 million prize

### 7:55 am Contestants Make the Grand March

The contest day starts bright and early. Breakfast is served at 6:30am. Finalists line up for the Grand March into the Competition Ballroom after breakfast. George and Sally Pillsbury, on the left, cheer finalists on as they make their way into the ballroom.

### 8 am Let the Contest Begin

Finalists take the supplies out of their mini-kitchens as the competition begins.

### 8:30 am The First Recipe Is Finished

The first finalist, Robin Ross, turns in her recipe, Granola Sweet Rolls on a Stick (page 38). It's a breakfast treat she created so kids could easily make it themselves.

### 10 am Most Finalists Are Still Cooking

### 1 pm The Contest Officially Ends

All recipes are now complete and the final dishes turned into the judges. Now the finalists wait while the judges sample all the delectable recipes!

### 6 pm Judges Decide While Contestants Dine

As the judges deliberate, debate and decide, the finalists board buses for a dinner and party at a Cuban café. Can't stay out too late though! A wake-up call will ring at 6 am because the winners will be announced early tomorrow morning!

### Next Morning, 7:30 am And the Winners Are . . .

All finalists are back in the grand ballroom anxiously awaiting the announcement of the 42nd Bake-Off® Contest Grand Prize Winner—every one of them wondering, "Will it be me?!"

# meet the $1 million winner

Anna Ginsberg of Austin, Texas, is named the Grand Prize Winner by TV personality Joy Behar. The judges say her recipe for Baked Chicken and Spinach Stuffing (page 128) is the best! In addition to the $1 million, she wins a set of stainless steel kitchen appliances.

For any Bake-Off® Contest winner, the days following the announcement are a whirlwind of media appearances. Just moments after the awards show, Anna is interviewed live on national TV and then talks to national radio networks and food reporters from around the country.

Later, she is whisked to the airport for a flight to New York City and appears on a national morning news show the next day, where she demonstrates her recipe to millions of TV viewers around the country. Life has never been quite the same since!

## everyone's a winner

Eight other finalists head home with their own $10,000 cash prize plus a brand new oven for their winning recipe in each of six food categories. In addition to the category awards, two special awards were given.

Anna Ginsberg gets the big news!

WAKE UP TO BREAKFAST™ Casual brunch or on-the-go breakfast ideas for busy weekday mornings or leisurely weekend brunches.

**Maria Baldwin** of Mesa, Arizona, won for her Rise 'n Shine Lattice Pizza (page 12).

DINNER MADE EASY™ Easy-to-make main dish recipes for busy weeknights, including recipes that can be prepared in 15 minutes or less (not including cooking, baking or cooling time) *or* that can be completely prepared and ready to serve in 30 minutes. No more than 10 ingredients were allowed (not including water, salt and pepper).

**Angela Buchanan** of Boulder, Colorado, won for her Cuban-Style Sandwiches with Green Chile au Jus (page 46).

BRAND NEW YOU Recipes for breakfast, lunch, dinner or snacks that reflect today's interest in healthier eating. For example, recipes could use techniques or ingredients that allow them to be lower in fat or calories, such as

reduced-fat products, fish or leaner cuts of meat; or recipes could include more "better for you" ingredients such as fruits or vegetables.

**Karen Mack** of Webster, New York, won for her Blackberry-Almond Bruschetta (page 82).

COOKING FOR TWO Easy-to-fix recipes with two servings for any meal of the day.

**Diane Leigh Kerekes** of Sapulpa, Oklahoma, won the Receta Rica Award for her Southwestern Chicken-Biscuit Pot Pie (page 116). Grand Prize Winner Anna Ginsberg was an entry from this category.

SIMPLE SNACKS Appetizers, snacks or treats to serve at casual gatherings with kids, family or friends.

**Ronna Farley** of Rockville, Maryland, won for her Choco–Peanut Butter Cups (page 152).

WEEKENDS MADE SPECIAL Special yet simple-to-prepare recipes to enjoy with family and friends on the weekend (not including recipes

for breakfast, brunch, appetizers or snacks).

**Laura Stensberg** of Marshfield, Wisconsin, won for her delectable Peanut Butter Truffle Tart (page 188).

AMERICA'S FAVORITE RECIPE AWARD Consumers voted online from January through February 2006 for the recipe they thought had the best taste, appearance, creativity and appeal from finalists' recipes.

**Mary Iovinelli Buescher's** Pineapple–Black Bean Enchiladas (page 98) was voted America's Favorite Recipe. Buescher hails from Bloomington, Minnesota.

RECETA RICA AWARD This award highlighted a recipe that creatively used Hispanic-inspired flavors, ingredients or techniques.

**Diane Leigh Kerekes** of Sapulpa, Oklahoma, won for her Southwestern Chicken-Biscuit Pot Pie (page 116). She also was the winner of the Cooking for Two category.

**Maria Baldwin** of Mesa, Arizona, was a winner when the judges sampled her Rise 'n Shine Lattice Pizza (page 12). She took home $10,000 and a brand new oven.

Rise 'n Shine Lattice Pizza

# chapter one

# wake up to breakfast™

Wake up to great ideas for an on-the-go breakfast on busy weekday mornings or for a leisurely weekend brunch.

## What's for Breakfast?

Americans are waking up to smoothies and parfaits, quick breads—including scones, old fashioned "crumb cake" and a wide variety of egg dishes, from French toast to frittatas.

Just because you're on the go doesn't mean you have to skip breakfast, especially with portable dishes like smoothies, shakes and breakfast snack mixes that were fast and easy to prepare.

America's cooks gave resounding approval to frozen fruits as a breakfast shortcut, with favorites including blueberry, raspberry, peach and strawberry.

Dipping sauces, many fruit-flavored, bring extra flavor and fun to breakfast.

Interesting ingredients that made an appearance in breakfast recipes were dried lavender, manchego cheese, orange-flavored dried cranberries and candied watermelon rind.

1 box (9 oz) frozen roasted potatoes with garlic and herbs

½ cup chives-and-onion cream cheese spread (from 8-oz container)

1 teaspoon Italian seasoning

2 eggs

¾ to 1 cup basil pesto (6 to 8 oz)

1 can (13.8 oz) refrigerated pizza crust

2 cups grated Asiago or Parmesan cheese (8 oz)

1 package or jar (3 oz) cooked real bacon bits

1 box (10.6 oz) refrigerated garlic breadsticks with herbs

## Maria Baldwin | Mesa, AZ

**Maria Baldwin** makes this pizza when her kids come home for the weekend. She said her interest in cooking began when she was in grade school: "I would spend hours looking through magazines and clipping recipes to save." Maria devoted plenty of time to cooking for her three younger brothers. Lucky them: In her first year in 4-H, Maria won a blue ribbon for gingersnap cookies.

# rise 'n shine lattice pizza

**8 servings** | Prep Time: **35 minutes** | Start to Finish: **1 hour 15 minutes**

1 Heat oven to 350°F. Cut small slit in center of pouch of potatoes. Microwave on High 2 to 3 minutes or just until warm; set aside. In small bowl, beat cream cheese, Italian seasoning and eggs with electric mixer on medium speed until well blended; set aside.

2 Line large cookie sheet with cooking parchment paper. Place pesto in small strainer over bowl to drain off excess oil. Lightly brush oil from pesto onto parchment paper. Unroll pizza crust dough on paper-lined cookie sheet; starting at center, press out dough into 14-inch square.

3 Spread pesto over dough to within 1 inch of edges; sprinkle cheese over pesto. Roll up edges of dough to make 11-inch square. Spoon potatoes evenly over cheese. Pour egg mixture around potatoes. Sprinkle with bacon bits.

4 Separate breadstick dough into 10 strips; set garlic butter aside. Twist and stretch each strip of dough over potatoes in lattice pattern, tucking ends of strips under pizza dough. Remove cover from reserved garlic butter; microwave on High 10 seconds to soften. Brush garlic butter over edges and strips of dough.

5 Bake 30 to 40 minutes or until edges are browned and center is set, covering with foil during last 10 minutes of baking if necessary to prevent excessive browning. Immediately remove from cookie sheet. Cut into rectangles to serve.

High Altitude **(3,500-6,500 ft): Heat oven to 375°F.**

**1 Serving:** Calories 630 (Calories from Fat 340); Total Fat 38g (Saturated Fat 14g; Trans Fat 0g); Cholesterol 125mg; Sodium 1740mg; Total Carbohydrate 47g (Dietary Fiber 4g; Sugars 6g); Protein 24g **% Daily Value:** Vitamin A 25%; Vitamin C 0%; Calcium 35%; Iron 20% **Exchanges:** 3 Starch, 2 Medium-Fat Meat, 5½ Fat **Carbohydrate Choices:** 3

**Quesadillas**

⅓ lb bulk pork sausage

6 eggs

2 tablespoons sour cream

2 tablespoons half-and-half

1 package (1.25 oz) taco seasoning mix

1 tablespoon butter or margarine

2 tablespoons finely chopped fresh chives

2 tablespoons finely chopped fresh cilantro

2 tablespoons chopped tomato

1 can (4.5 oz) chopped green chiles

1 package (11.5 oz) flour tortillas for burritos, 8 inch (8 tortillas)

½ cup shredded Cheddar cheese (2 oz)

½ cup shredded Monterey Jack cheese (2 oz)

**Toppings**

2 to 4 tablespoons finely chopped fresh chives

2 to 4 tablespoons taco sauce

2 to 4 tablespoons sour cream

Jane Ozment | Purcell, OK

**Jane Ozment**'s recipe combines typical breakfast ingredients with Mexican flavors. Her husband tried it and "loved it." Good thing, she serves the quesadillas to him every week or two. Jane began cooking at an early age and by age 10 she was regularly helping in the kitchen.

# breakfast quesadillas

**4 servings (2 quesadillas each)**  |  Prep Time: **30 minutes**  |  Start to Finish: **35 minutes**

1  In 12-inch nonstick skillet, cook sausage over medium heat, stirring frequently, until browned and no longer pink. Remove sausage from skillet; drain on paper towels. Wipe skillet clean with paper towels; set aside. Meanwhile, in medium bowl, lightly beat eggs, 2 tablespoons sour cream, the half-and-half and taco seasoning mix with wire whisk until well blended.

2  In 10-inch nonstick skillet, melt butter over medium heat. Add egg mixture; cook 2 to 4 minutes, stirring frequently, until mixture is very moist. Stir in cooked sausage, 2 tablespoons chives, the cilantro, tomato and chiles. Cook 1 to 2 minutes longer or until egg mixture is set but still moist. Remove from heat.

3  Place tortillas on work surface. Top half of each tortilla with 2 to 3 tablespoons egg mixture; sprinkle each with 1 tablespoon of each of the cheeses. Fold untopped half of tortillas over egg mixture.

4  Heat same 12-inch skillet over medium heat. Place 2 quesadillas in skillet; cook 30 to 45 seconds on each side or until crisp and lightly browned. Remove from skillet; place on serving plate. Repeat with remaining quesadillas. With pizza cutter or sharp knife, cut each quesadilla into wedges. Top each serving (2 quesadillas) with about ½ tablespoon each of chives, taco sauce and sour cream.

High Altitude (3,500–6,500 ft): No change.

2 **Quesadillas:** Calories 640 (Calories from Fat 330); Total Fat 37g (Saturated Fat 16g; Trans Fat 0.5g); Cholesterol 380mg; Sodium 2030mg; Total Carbohydrate 52g (Dietary Fiber 0g; Sugars 3g); Protein 27g **% Daily Value:** Vitamin A 25%; Vitamin C 10%; Calcium 40%; Iron 25% **Exchanges:** 2½ Starch, 1 Other Carbohydrate, 2½ Medium-Fat Meat, 4½ Fat **Carbohydrate Choices:** 3½

1 bag (19 oz) frozen roasted potatoes with broccoli and cheese sauce

1 refrigerated pie crust (from 15-oz box), softened as directed on box

4 eggs

⅔ cup whipping cream

7 slices bacon, cooked, crumbled (about ⅓ cup)

1 cup finely shredded Parmesan cheese (4 oz)

1 cup finely shredded Cheddar cheese (4 oz)

½ teaspoon dried basil leaves

½ teaspoon pepper

¼ teaspoon parsley flakes

⅛ teaspoon salt, if desired

1 teaspoon finely chopped fresh chives

# broccoli, potato and bacon quiche

**8 servings** | Prep Time: **20 minutes** | Start to Finish: **1 hour**

1 Heat oven to 350°F. Cook frozen potatoes with broccoli and cheese sauce in microwave as directed on bag.

2 Meanwhile, place pie crust in 9-inch glass pie plate as directed on box for One-Crust Filled Pie.

3 In large bowl, beat eggs and whipping cream with wire whisk until well blended. Stir in cooked potato mixture and remaining ingredients except chives. Pour filling into crust-lined plate; spread evenly. Sprinkle chives over filling.

4 Bake 30 to 40 minutes or until edge of filling is light golden brown and knife inserted in center comes out clean. Let stand 5 minutes before serving.

High Altitude (3,500–6,500 ft): Heat oven to 375°F. Bake 33 to 43 minutes.

1 **Serving:** Calories 410 (Calories from Fat 260); Total Fat 29g (Saturated Fat 14g; Trans Fat 0g); Cholesterol 165mg; Sodium 880mg; Total Carbohydrate 21g (Dietary Fiber 1g; Sugars 3g); Protein 17g % **Daily Value:** Vitamin A 15%; Vitamin C 4%; Calcium 30%; Iron 4% **Exchanges:** 1½ Starch, 1½ Medium-Fat Meat, 4 Fat **Carbohydrate Choices:** 1½

Tanya Nicole Margala |
Newport Beach, CA

When **Tanya Nicole Margala** needs a recipe idea, she turns to her taste buds . . . and to potatoes. "I wanted a new way to eat my favorite food—potatoes—with eggs," she said. Her quiche is an easy "faux gourmet" dish ideal for a casual breakfast or brunch or for occasions when you want to impress your guests.

1 tablespoon olive oil

½ teaspoon chili oil

1 small boneless skinless chicken breast (4 oz), cut into thin bite-size strips

¼ medium green bell pepper, cut into julienne strips (2 × ¼ inch)

¼ medium red bell pepper, cut into julienne strips (2 × ¼ inch)

¼ medium yellow bell pepper, cut into julienne strips (2 × ¼ inch)

¼ teaspoon garlic salt

¼ teaspoon ground cinnamon

¼ teaspoon chili powder

¼ teaspoon black pepper

⅛ teaspoon ground red pepper (cayenne)

1 teaspoon fresh lime juice

4 eggs

1 cup whipping cream

½ teaspoon salt

1 can (4.5 oz) chopped green chiles

1 cup shredded Cheddar cheese (4 oz)

1 cup shredded Monterey Jack cheese (4 oz)

1 refrigerated pie crust (from 15-oz box), softened as directed on box

1 cup organic or chunky-style salsa

## Mary Beth Schultz | Valparaiso, IN

Not even a broken leg could stop **Mary Beth Schultz** from preparing this quiche. In fact, inventing recipes kept her busy during her recovery. She served this dish to her family, who loved it. Mary Beth tends to "ad lib most recipes," so she credited her daughter with giving her the most valuable advice: "Write it down."

# chicken fajita quiche

**8 servings** | Prep Time: **20 minutes** | Start to Finish: **1 hour 25 minutes**

1 Heat oven to 375°F. In 10-inch skillet, heat olive and chili oil over medium-high heat. Add chicken; cook and stir 2 to 3 minutes or until lightly browned and no longer pink in center. Reserve several bell pepper strips of each color for garnish; add remaining strips to skillet. Cook about 1 minute, stirring frequently, until slightly softened. Sprinkle with garlic salt, cinnamon, chili powder, pepper, red pepper and lime juice; stir to mix. Remove from heat; cool slightly.

2 In large bowl, beat eggs, whipping cream, salt and green chiles with wire whisk until blended. Gently stir in both cheeses. Stir chicken mixture into egg mixture.

3 Place pie crust in 10-inch quiche dish or 9-inch glass pie plate as directed on box for One-Crust Filled Pie. Pour chicken mixture into crust-lined pan. Arrange reserved bell pepper strips in pinwheel fashion over filling.

4 Bake 35 to 45 minutes or until knife inserted in center comes out clean and filling is golden brown. Let stand 15 to 20 minutes on wire rack before serving. Serve salsa over individual servings.

High Altitude (3,500–6,500 ft): In step 2, stir 2 tablespoons flour into egg mixture. Bake 48 to 52 minutes.

**1 Serving:** Calories 400 (Calories from Fat 270); Total Fat 30g (Saturated Fat 15g; Trans Fat 0g); Cholesterol 180mg; Sodium 700mg; Total Carbohydrate 18g (Dietary Fiber 0g; Sugars 3g); Protein 14g **% Daily Value:** Vitamin A 20%; Vitamin C 20%; Calcium 25%; Iron 4% **Exchanges:** 1 Starch, 1½ Medium-Fat Meat, 4½ Fat **Carbohydrate Choices:** 1

5 frozen buttermilk waffles (from 12-oz bag), thawed

2 cans (8 oz each) crushed pineapple in juice

1½ cups finely chopped bananas (2 medium)

4 eggs

⅔ cup granulated sugar

5 tablespoons packed brown sugar

3 pouches (6 bars) oats 'n honey crunchy granola bars (from 8.9-oz box), crushed (heaping 1 cup)*

½ cup chopped macadamia nuts

3 tablespoons all-purpose flour

¼ cup butter or margarine, softened

1 jar (10 oz) strawberry spreadable fruit

Whipped cream, if desired

*To easily crush granola bars, do not unwrap; use rolling pin to crush bars.

### Diane Toomey | Allentown, PA

"This recipe began as an adaptation of a favorite recipe we often have on holidays called Baked Pineapple," said **Diane Toomey**. She replaced the bread with waffles, added bananas, topping and strawberry sauce, and, voilà: her family all asked for more. With four kids, time is always at a premium. Diane saves time by incorporating prepared foods into her home cooking.

# tropical waffle bake

**6 servings** | Prep Time: **25 minutes** | Start to Finish: **1 hour 10 minutes**

1 Heat oven to 350°F. Spray 8-inch square (2-quart) glass baking dish with cooking spray. Break waffles into 1- to 2-inch pieces; place in bottom of baking dish. Drain pineapple, reserving juice in small bowl; set pineapple aside. Gently stir bananas into juice to coat. With slotted spoon, place bananas evenly over waffles; discard any remaining juice.

2 In medium bowl, beat eggs, granulated sugar and 2 tablespoons of the brown sugar with wire whisk until blended. Stir in drained pineapple. Pour mixture over waffles and bananas in dish. In another medium bowl, mix crushed granola bars, nuts, flour, remaining 3 tablespoons brown sugar and the butter until crumbly; sprinkle over top.

3 Bake 30 to 35 minutes or until knife inserted in center comes out clean. Cool 10 minutes.

4 To serve, in small microwavable bowl, microwave spreadable fruit on High 1 minute. Stir; if necessary, continue to microwave on High in 15-second increments until melted and smooth. Cut into 6 servings. Top each serving with about 2 tablespoons warm fruit spread and 1 to 2 tablespoons whipped cream.

High Altitude (3,500–6,500 ft): Heat oven to 375°F.

1 Serving: Calories 700 (Calories from Fat 210); Total Fat 24g (Saturated Fat 8g; Trans Fat 1g); Cholesterol 160mg; Sodium 410mg; Total Carbohydrate 111g (Dietary Fiber 7g; Sugars 80g); Protein 11g **% Daily Value:** Vitamin A 20%; Vitamin C 10%; Calcium 8%; Iron 20% **Exchanges:** 1 Starch, 1 Fruit, 5½ Other Carbohydrate, 1 High-Fat Meat, 3 Fat **Carbohydrate Choices:** 7½

### Pancakes

2 boxes (16.4 oz each) frozen microwave pancakes (24 pancakes)

2 tablespoons butter or margarine, softened

3 eggs

1 cup half-and-half

¼ cup maple-flavored syrup with butter

½ teaspoon ground cinnamon

2 containers (6 oz each) fat-free banana cream pie yogurt

4 medium bananas, cut diagonally into ¼-inch-thick slices

½ cup chopped pecans

### Garnishes

¾ cup extra-creamy whipped topping with real cream

12 diagonal slices bananas (¼ inch thick)

¾ cup maple-flavored syrup with butter

½ teaspoon ground cinnamon

2 tablespoons chopped pecans, if desired

Additional ground cinnamon, if desired

Pam Ivbuls | Omaha, NE

Whenever **Pam Ivbuls** arrives home from a stressful day, she turns on the oven. "Baking helps me to relax," she said. This recipe idea came to her late one evening. "My creative juices wouldn't let me fall asleep until I had come up with a likable version." Pam's kitchen is home to 26 Pillsbury Doughboy® figures, autographed pictures of famous chefs and a complete set of Bake-Off® cookbooks dating back to the first edition from 1949.

# banana-pecan-pancake bake

**12 servings**  |  Prep Time: **20 minutes**  |  Start to Finish: **1 hour 25 minutes**

1  Heat oven to 350°F. Remove frozen pancakes from boxes; unwrap and carefully separate. Set aside to partially thaw. With small pastry brush, coat bottom and sides of 15 × 10 × 1-inch pan with softened butter.

2  In 5-cup blender or large food processor, place eggs, half-and-half, ¼ cup syrup, ½ teaspoon cinnamon and the yogurt; cover and blend on low speed 10 seconds until smooth. If necessary, scrape down sides of blender with rubber spatula and blend 5 to 10 seconds longer. Set aside.

3  Place 12 of the pancakes in 4 rows of 3 pancakes each, overlapping slightly if necessary, in pan. Pour 1½ cups yogurt mixture evenly over pancakes (if necessary, use small spoon to coat surface of each pancake with yogurt mixture).

4  Place banana slices in single layer over pancakes. Place remaining 12 pancakes over banana-topped pancakes. Pour remaining yogurt mixture evenly over all pancakes. With large turkey baster, coat pancakes evenly with yogurt mixture from pan. Let stand 10 minutes to allow yogurt mixture to soak into pancakes. With baster, coat pancakes again with yogurt mixture from pan. Let stand 5 minutes longer. Sprinkle ½ cup pecans evenly over top.

5  Bake 30 to 40 minutes or until edges are set and light golden brown. Let stand 10 minutes before serving.

6  Cut into 12 servings; place on individual plates. Top each with 1 tablespoon whipped topping, 1 banana slice and 1 tablespoon syrup; sprinkle each with dash cinnamon and ½ teaspoon pecans. Sprinkle edge of each plate with additional cinnamon.

High Altitude (3,500–6,500 ft): No change.

1 **Serving:** Calories 430 (Calories from Fat 120); Total Fat 13g (Saturated Fat 5g; Trans Fat 1g); Cholesterol 80mg; Sodium 520mg; Total Carbohydrate 70g (Dietary Fiber 2g; Sugars 29g); Protein 8g  **% Daily Value:** Vitamin A 8%; Vitamin C 4%; Calcium 15%; Iron 10% **Exchanges:** 2½ Starch, 2 Other Carbohydrate, 2½ Fat **Carbohydrate Choices:** 4½

2 cups Reese's® Puffs® cereal

4 eggs

¼ cup milk

1 teaspoon vanilla

12 tablespoons creamy peanut butter

12 slices white or wheat sandwich bread or
slightly firm bread

4 peanut butter crunchy granola bars
(2 pouches from 8.9-oz box), finely
crushed (¾ cup)*

6 tablespoons marshmallow creme
(from 7-oz jar)

Reese's® is a registered trademark of
Hershey Foods Corporation.

*To easily crush granola bars, do not
unwrap; use rolling pin to crush bars.

Kendra Norris | Crossville, TN

"My kids' two favorite foods are French toast and peanut butter—marshmallow sandwiches," said **Kendra Norris**. She combined those favorites for a sweet breakfast treat her kids love. She always wanted to enter the Bake-Off® Contest, and this time she decided to give it a shot. When Kendra learned she was a finalist, she says she could barely contain herself. "I ran down the hallway jumping and screaming! My kids asked, 'What's wrong with you?'"

# granola-peanut butter french toast

**6 servings**  |  Prep Time: **20 minutes**  |  Start to Finish: **20 minutes**

1  Place cereal in gallon-size resealable food-storage plastic bag. With flat side of meat mallet or rolling pin, crush cereal until very fine, making 1⅓ cups crumbs. Place on large plate; set aside.

2  In medium bowl, beat eggs, milk and vanilla with wire whisk until well blended. Spread 2 tablespoons peanut butter on each of 6 slices of bread. Sprinkle each with about 2 tablespoons crushed granola bars.

3  Spread 1 tablespoon marshmallow creme on each of remaining 6 slices of bread. Top peanut butter–spread bread with marshmallow-spread bread, marshmallow side down, making 6 sandwiches.

4  Spray griddle or 12-inch skillet with cooking spray; heat to 350°F or over medium heat. Dip each side of each sandwich into egg mixture, then coat each side with cereal crumbs; place on hot griddle. Cook 2 to 4 minutes on each side or until golden brown. Serve warm; if desired, serve with maple- or chocolate-flavored syrup.

High Altitude (3,500–6,500 ft): If using electric griddle or skillet, heat to 375°F.

1 Serving: Calories 530 (Calories from Fat 230); Total Fat 26g (Saturated Fat 5g; Trans Fat 0.5g); Cholesterol 140mg; Sodium 690mg; Total Carbohydrate 57g (Dietary Fiber 4g; Sugars 20g); Protein 19g  % Daily Value: Vitamin A 8%; Vitamin C 2%; Calcium 15%; Iron 30%  Exchanges: 2½ Starch, 1 Other Carbohydrate, 1½ High-Fat Meat, 2½ Fat Carbohydrate Choices: 4

1 bag (10 oz) organic frozen blueberries

½ cup small-curd 2% reduced-fat cottage cheese

2 tablespoons granulated sugar

½ teaspoon grated lemon peel

¼ to ½ teaspoon ground nutmeg

¼ to ½ teaspoon ground cinnamon

4 oz ⅓-less-fat cream cheese (Neufchâtel), softened

1 container (6 oz) light blueberry patch fat-free yogurt

1 package (11.5 oz) flour tortillas for burritos, 8 inch (8 tortillas)

1 tablespoon butter or margarine

¼ cup blueberry syrup

Powdered sugar, if desired

Lemon slices, if desired

# blueberry burrito blintzes

**8 servings**  |  Prep Time: **30 minutes**  |  Start to Finish: **30 minutes**

1  Thaw blueberries as directed on bag; drain, reserving liquid. In medium bowl, mix cottage cheese, sugar, lemon peel, nutmeg, cinnamon, cream cheese and yogurt until well blended. Gently stir in drained blueberries.

2  Place large sheet of waxed paper on work surface. For each blintz, place 1 flour tortilla on waxed paper. Spoon about ⅓ cup yogurt mixture in center. With pastry brush, moisten outer edge of tortilla with reserved blueberry liquid. Fold opposite sides of tortilla over filling, ends meeting in center; fold remaining 2 sides of tortilla over each other.

3  In 12-inch nonstick skillet, melt ½ tablespoon of the butter over medium heat. Cook 4 blintzes at a time, seam side down, about 2 minutes on each side until golden brown. Place blintzes, seam side down, on serving platter; drizzle with syrup. Sprinkle with powdered sugar; garnish with lemon slices.

High Altitude (3,500–6,500 ft): Cook blintzes about 5 minutes on each side.

1 Serving: Calories 300 (Calories from Fat 80); Total Fat 9g (Saturated Fat 4g; Trans Fat 0g); Cholesterol 15mg; Sodium 460mg; Total Carbohydrate 45g (Dietary Fiber 1g; Sugars 17g); Protein 8g  % Daily Value: Vitamin A 6%; Vitamin C 4%; Calcium 10%; Iron 8%  Exchanges: 2 Starch, 1 Other Carbohydrate, 1½ Fat  Carbohydrate Choices: 3

Kathy Anne Sepich  |  Gresham, OR

Cheese blintzes are one of **Kathy Anne Sepich**'s family's favorite breakfast foods. "I tried to think of an easier way to prepare them and that's where the idea for the flour tortilla came in." On becoming a finalist: "Next to having babies and getting married, it's the most exciting thing that's ever happened to me!" At age nine, Kathy's cake won first place in a 4-H contest.

## Pudding

1 bag (12.4 oz) frozen French dinner rolls

6 eggs

½ cup maple-flavored or real maple syrup

¾ cup sugar

1½ teaspoons baking powder

1 pint (2 cups) half-and-half

1 cup milk

¼ cup butter or margarine, melted

½ cup cream cheese creamy ready-to-spread
    frosting (from 16-oz container)

1 container (6 oz) French vanilla
    low-fat yogurt

**Garnishes, if desired**

Vanilla ice cream

Fresh mint sprigs

Powdered sugar

Beth Royals | Richmond, VA

"I've loved to cook for as
long as I can remember,"
said **Beth Royals.** When
she saw crusty French
frozen dinner rolls at the
grocery, she wondered how they
would taste in a bread pudding—her
favorite. The verdict, according to
her seven-year-old: "Yummy." Her
cooking inspiration is her dad, who
is "a creative, experimental cook who
takes meticulous notes."

# vermont maple bread pudding

**12 servings**  |  Prep Time: **25 minutes**  |  Start to Finish: **1 hour 35 minutes**

1  Heat oven to 350°F. Spray 13 × 9-inch pan with cooking spray. Let frozen
rolls stand at room temperature 10 minutes. Cut each roll into 12 pieces;
place in large bowl.

2  In another large bowl, slightly beat eggs. Reserve 1 tablespoon of the syrup
in small microwavable bowl; add remaining syrup to eggs. Stir in sugar,
baking powder, half-and-half, milk and melted butter until well blended.
Pour mixture over roll pieces in bowl; stir to coat well. Pour mixture into
pan, pressing bread into liquid with back of spoon. Let stand 5 minutes;
press down bread again.

3  Bake 45 to 55 minutes or until top is golden brown and knife inserted in
center comes out clean. Cool 20 minutes before serving.

4  To reserved tablespoon syrup, stir in frosting and yogurt. Microwave
on High about 20 seconds or until melted. Stir; pour over warm bread
pudding and spread to cover. Cut into 12 servings. Serve warm with ice
cream; garnish with mint and sprinkle with powdered sugar.

High Altitude (3,500–6,500 ft): Bake 50 to 60 minutes.

**1 Serving:** Calories 380 (Calories from Fat 140); Total Fat 16g (Saturated Fat 8g; Trans Fat 0g); Cholesterol 135mg;
Sodium 360mg; Total Carbohydrate 50g (Dietary Fiber 0g; Sugars 30g); Protein 9g  **% Daily Value:** Vitamin A 10%;
Vitamin C 0%; Calcium 15%; Iron 8%  **Exchanges:** 1½ Starch, 2 Other Carbohydrate, ½ Medium-Fat Meat, 2½ Fat
**Carbohydrate Choices:** 3

4 pecan crunch crunchy granola bars
    (2 pouches from 8.9-oz box), crushed
    (¾ cup)*

¼ cup chopped pecans

1 teaspoon ground cinnamon

1 cup whipping cream

½ cup packed light brown sugar

2 cans (17.5 oz each) large refrigerated
    cinnamon rolls with icing

1 medium Granny Smith apple, peeled,
    coarsely chopped (about 1¼ cups)

*To easily crush granola bars, do not
unwrap; use rolling pin to crush bars.

Lisa McDaniel | Highland, IL

**Lisa McDaniel**, mother of two and a lifelong fan of the Chicago Bears, said the Bake-Off® Contest is like the "Super Bowl of baking." Her recipe is quick and easy and makes breakfast "extra special because it's so rich, gooey and delicious."

# gooey caramel apple pull-aparts

**12 servings**  |  Prep Time: **10 minutes**  |  Start to Finish: **1 hour 20 minutes**

1  Heat oven to 350°F. Spray 12-cup fluted tube cake pan with cooking spray. In small bowl, mix crushed granola bars, pecans and ½ teaspoon of the cinnamon. Sprinkle mixture evenly in bottom of pan.

2  In large bowl, mix whipping cream, brown sugar and remaining ½ teaspoon cinnamon. Separate both cans of dough into 10 rolls; set icing aside. Cut each roll into quarters. Stir roll pieces and apple into whipping cream mixture to coat. Spoon mixture into pan; spread evenly.

3  Bake 50 to 60 minutes or until deep golden brown. Immediately place heatproof serving plate or platter upside down over pan; turn plate and pan over (do not remove pan). Cool 5 minutes. Remove pan; scrape any remaining topping in pan onto coffee cake. Cool 5 minutes longer. Drizzle reserved icing over top. Serve warm.

High Altitude (3,500–6,500 ft): Heat oven to 375°F. Bake 40 to 50 minutes.

1 Serving: Calories 420 (Calories from Fat 160); Total Fat 18g (Saturated Fat 7g; Trans Fat 2.5g); Cholesterol 20mg; Sodium 600mg; Total Carbohydrate 60g (Dietary Fiber 2g; Sugars 32g); Protein 6g  % Daily Value: Vitamin A 4%; Vitamin C 0%; Calcium 4%; Iron 10% Exchanges: 2 Starch, 2 Other Carbohydrate, 3½ Fat Carbohydrate Choices: 4

1 can (12.4 oz) refrigerated cinnamon rolls
  with icing

8 banana nut crunchy granola bars
  (4 pouches from 8.9-oz box), crushed
  (1½ cups)*

4 eggs

¾ cup fat-free (skim) milk

1 can (14 oz) fat-free sweetened condensed
  milk (not evaporated)

3 medium bananas, cut into 1-inch pieces

1 bag (10 oz) organic frozen blueberries,
  thawed

1 aerosol can (7 oz) fat-free whipped cream
  topping

*To easily crush granola bars, do not
unwrap; use rolling pin to crush bars.

Carolyn Roberts | Los Angeles, CA

**Carolyn Roberts**
concocted this finalist
recipe based on the
French toast prepared at
two of her favorite
restaurants. She served it on her
husband's birthday and received raves
from friends who previously owned a
restaurant. Diagnosed with multiple
sclerosis at age 25, Carolyn develops
programs on spirituality and wellness
for people with MS.

# blueberry-banana-granola french toast

**8 servings** | Prep Time: **10 minutes** | Start to Finish: **1 hour 10 minutes**

1 Heat oven to 350°F (325°F for dark pan). Spray 13 × 9-inch pan or
12 × 2-inch round cake pan with butter-flavor or regular cooking spray.
Separate dough into 8 rolls; set icing aside. Cut each roll into quarters;
arrange evenly in pan. Sprinkle ¾ cup of the crushed granola bars evenly
over dough pieces.

2 In large food processor or 5-cup blender, place eggs, milk and condensed
milk; cover and process 1 minute. Add bananas; cover and process
1 minute. Pour egg mixture over dough in pan. Sprinkle with remaining
¾ cup crushed granola bars.

3 Bake 35 to 45 minutes or until golden brown and set in center. Spoon
and spread reserved icing over warm rolls. Cool 15 minutes before serving.

4 To serve, spoon baked French toast into shallow bowls or cut into
8 servings. Top each serving with 3 tablespoons blueberries; garnish with
2 tablespoons whipped cream topping.

High Altitude (3,500–6,500 ft): Heat oven to 375°F. Add 2 tablespoons flour to
ingredients in blender. Bake 30 to 40 minutes.

1 Serving: Calories 500 (Calories from Fat 100); Total Fat 11g (Saturated Fat 3g; Trans Fat 2g); Cholesterol 110mg;
Sodium 510mg; Total Carbohydrate 87g (Dietary Fiber 3g; Sugars 60g); Protein 13g  % Daily Value: Vitamin A 6%;
Vitamin C 6%; Calcium 20%; Iron 10%  Exchanges: 2 Starch, 1 Fruit, 3 Other Carbohydrate, 1 Medium-Fat Meat, 1 Fat
Carbohydrate Choices: 6

½ cup salted roasted macadamia nuts

⅓ cup packed brown sugar

2 packages (3 oz each) cream cheese, softened

1 cup organic frozen raspberries (from 10-oz bag), thawed as directed on bag, drained and liquid reserved

1 can (16.3 oz) large refrigerated buttermilk flaky biscuits

⅓ cup flaked coconut

# raspberry-nut dreams

**16 sweet rolls**  |  Prep Time: **25 minutes**  |  Start to Finish: **55 minutes**

1 Heat oven to 350°F. Lightly spray 16 regular-size muffin cups with cooking spray. In food processor, process macadamia nuts with on-and-off motions until coarsely chopped. Add brown sugar; process until combined. Place in small bowl; set aside.

2 In same food processor, process cream cheese, 2 tablespoons nut mixture and 1 to 2 tablespoons reserved raspberry liquid until smooth.

3 Separate dough into 8 biscuits; separate each into 2 layers, making a total of 16 rounds. Lightly press each round in bottom and up side of muffin cup. Spoon about ½ tablespoon cream cheese mixture into each dough-lined cup. Top each evenly with raspberries, 1 tablespoon remaining nut mixture and 1 teaspoon coconut.

4 Bake 14 to 22 minutes or until coconut is lightly browned. Cool in pan 5 minutes before serving.

High Altitude (3,500–6,500 ft): No change.

1 Sweet Roll: Calories 190 (Calories from Fat 100); Total Fat 11g (Saturated Fat 4g; Trans Fat 2g); Cholesterol 10mg; Sodium 320mg; Total Carbohydrate 19g (Dietary Fiber 2g; Sugars 8g); Protein 3g % Daily Value: Vitamin A 2%; Vitamin C 4%; Calcium 2%; Iron 6% Exchanges: 1 Starch, ½ Other Carbohydrate, 2 Fat Carbohydrate Choices: 1

Kathy Sweeton  |  Long Beach, CA

**Kathy Sweeton** likes the fact that her recipe is simple to prepare. So does her husband—especially since he's on kitchen clean-up duty. His cooking advice to her is "keep it simple." With just a few ingredients to this fruity breakfast treat, that's not a problem. Because it's so easy to make, Kathy often brings it to treat days at the school where she teaches.

**Pastries**

½ cup unseasoned dry bread crumbs

2 to 2½ tablespoons golden raisins

2 tablespoons packed light brown sugar

2 tablespoons flaked coconut

2 tablespoons finely chopped walnuts

1 egg white

½ teaspoon vanilla

5 tablespoons apricot fruit spread

1 tablespoon powdered sugar

1 can (10.1 oz) large refrigerated crescent dinner rolls

**Glaze**

½ cup powdered sugar

⅛ teaspoon vanilla

1½ to 1¾ teaspoons water

---

Arlene Swiatek Gillen | Holland, NY

Count on **Arlene Swiatek Gillen** to come up with quick and easy recipes that look like they took hours to prepare. She's a decorative artist whose ornament was among those chosen for display on the official White House Christmas Tree in 2004. Now she and her husband regularly enjoy these "better-than-bakery" goodies with a cup of coffee and the morning paper.

# fruit and nut pastries

**7 pastries**  |  Prep Time: **25 minutes**  |  Start to Finish: **1 hour**

1 Heat oven to 350°F. Line large cookie sheet with foil; lightly spray foil with cooking spray. In medium bowl, mix bread crumbs, raisins, brown sugar, coconut and walnuts.

2 In small bowl, beat egg white and ½ teaspoon vanilla with wire whisk about 30 seconds or until frothy. Stir into brown sugar mixture until well blended. In another small bowl, place fruit spread; stir with fork to break up any large pieces of fruit.

3 Cut 16 × 12-inch sheet of waxed paper; place on work surface. With fine strainer, sift 1 tablespoon powdered sugar onto paper. Unroll dough onto sugared paper; press into 14 × 7-inch rectangle, firmly pressing perforations to seal. Spread fruit spread over dough to edges. With pizza cutter, cut dough in half crosswise to make 2 (7-inch) squares.

4 Top 1 dough square with brown sugar mixture, spreading evenly over fruit spread to edges of dough. With waxed paper, lift remaining dough square and turn upside down over brown sugar mixture; lightly press. Remove paper. With pizza cutter, cut filled dough into 7 (1-inch-wide) strips. Carefully twist each strip 3 times; shape into loose knot, tucking ends under (dough will be sticky). Place 3 inches apart on cookie sheet.

5 Bake 17 to 25 minutes or until golden brown. Remove pastries from cookie sheet; place on wire racks. Cool 15 minutes.

6 In small bowl, blend ½ cup powdered sugar, ⅛ teaspoon vanilla and enough water for desired drizzling consistency. Drizzle glaze over cooled pastries. If desired, place small bowl of softened butter in center of serving platter; arrange pastries on platter around bowl.

High Altitude (3,500–6,500 ft): Bake 18 to 21 minutes.

1 Pastry: Calories 310 (Calories from Fat 100); Total Fat 11g (Saturated Fat 2.5g; Trans Fat 2g); Cholesterol 0mg; Sodium 390mg; Total Carbohydrate 48g (Dietary Fiber 2g; Sugars 26g); Protein 5g  % **Daily Value:** Vitamin A 0%; Vitamin C 0%; Calcium 2%; Iron 10%  **Exchanges:** 1½ Starch, 1½ Other Carbohydrate, 2 Fat  **Carbohydrate Choices:** 3

1 can (7.3 oz) refrigerated cinnamon rolls
with icing (5 rolls)

1 container (6 oz) French vanilla
low-fat yogurt

4 cinnamon crunchy granola bars
(2 pouches from 8.9-oz box), finely
crushed (¾ cup)*

1 large banana

5 round wooden sticks with one pointed
end (10 inch)

*To easily crush granola bars, do not
unwrap; use rolling pin to crush bars.

Robin Ross | St Petersburg, FL

How did **Robin Ross**
come up with her idea
for this recipe? "I was
thinking of something
that might be used in
a camp-out," she said. Robin's
breakfast dish is a snap to make with
few ingredients. It can be eaten at
the table or "on the go."

# granola sweet rolls on a stick

**5 servings (1 roll and 1½ tablespoons sauce each)** | Prep Time: **15 minutes** | Start to
Finish: **40 minutes**

1 Heat oven to 375°F. Grease large cookie sheet with shortening or cooking
spray. Separate dough into 5 rolls; set icing aside. Place rolls on cookie
sheet. With sharp knife or 1- to 1¼-inch cookie cutter, cut hole in center
of each roll; set roll cutouts aside.

2 Place yogurt in shallow bowl. Place crushed granola bars in another shallow bowl. Peel banana; cut off small slice from each end and cut remaining
banana into 5 equal pieces. Place banana pieces in yogurt; stir with spoon
until coated. Roll banana pieces in crushed granola bars to coat well. Place
1 coated banana piece in hole in each roll, making hole larger if necessary.
Set remaining yogurt aside.

3 Thread stick through side of each roll, through banana and out other side
of roll. Slide roll down stick about ⅓ of length. Thread 1 reserved roll
cutout onto stick.

4 Bake 12 to 17 minutes or until golden brown and dough around center of
roll is no longer doughy. Cool 5 minutes. Meanwhile, stir reserved icing
into remaining yogurt for sauce. If desired, cut off sharp ends from sticks
with kitchen scissors. Loosen rolls and remove from cookie sheet. Serve
with yogurt sauce for dipping.

High Altitude (3,500–6,500 ft): No change.

**1 Serving:** Calories 280 (Calories from Fat 70); Total Fat 8g (Saturated Fat 2g; Trans Fat 2g); Cholesterol 0mg; Sodium 430mg;
Total Carbohydrate 46g (Dietary Fiber 2g; Sugars 24g); Protein 6g **% Daily Value:** Vitamin A 4%; Vitamin C 2%; Calcium 6%;
Iron 6% **Exchanges:** 1½ Starch, ½ Other Carbohydrate, 1½ Fat **Carbohydrate Choices:** 3

**Filling**

1 egg

2 tablespoons milk

1 cup unseasoned dry bread crumbs

2 tablespoons granulated sugar

2 tablespoons butter, melted

¼ cup water

2 teaspoons almond extract

**Glaze**

½ cup granulated sugar

¼ cup water

1 tablespoon light corn syrup

**Rolls**

1 can (8 oz) refrigerated crescent
   dinner rolls

⅓ to ½ cup sliced almonds

**Icing**

1 cup powdered sugar

2 tablespoons water

Maureen McBride | San Jose, CA

**Maureen McBride**
wanted to make "bakery-tasting" bear claws with faster, easier ingredients. She reported feeling flabbergasted, giddy and shocked when she got "the call" from a Bake-Off® Contest staffer. "Two years ago, I created some recipes and tested them on my friends," said Maureen. "Their feedback: 'Keep your day job.' I had better luck with recipe creations this year."

# crescent bear claws

**6 bear claws** | Prep Time: **20 minutes** | Start to Finish: **45 minutes**

1 Heat oven to 375°F. Line cookie sheet with cooking parchment paper. In medium bowl, beat egg lightly with wire whisk. Place half of egg (about 1½ tablespoons) in custard cup; beat in milk until blended and set aside. To remaining egg in bowl, stir in remaining filling ingredients until well blended.

2 Meanwhile, in 1-quart heavy saucepan, mix glaze ingredients. Heat to boiling. Remove from heat; cool while making rolls.

3 On lightly floured work surface, unroll dough; press into 12 × 8-inch rectangle, firmly pressing perforations to seal. Spoon filling into 12 × 2-inch strip lengthwise down center ⅓ of dough. Fold ⅓ of dough over filling. Fold filling-topped section over last ⅓ of dough so seam is on bottom of folded dough. With hand, gently flatten 1-inch-wide strip of dough along one long side of folded dough. Cut folded dough crosswise into 6 (2-inch) pastries. Along flattened edge of each pastry, cut 1-inch-long cuts about ½ inch apart.

4 Lightly brush egg-milk mixture over each pastry. Place almonds on plate; invert each pastry onto almonds and press gently so almonds stick to dough. Place almond side up on cookie sheet, spreading each cut slightly to form claw shape. Sprinkle remaining almonds over top of pastries.

5 Bake 15 to 18 minutes or until golden brown. Remove to wire rack; cool 5 minutes. Drizzle cooled glaze over each pastry. In another small bowl, mix icing ingredients until smooth (if icing is too thick, add ½ teaspoon water at a time until drizzling consistency). Drizzle icing over cooled pastries.

High Altitude (3,500-6,500 ft): Bake 14 to 17 minutes.

1 Bear Claw: Calories 470 (Calories from Fat 150); Total Fat 16g (Saturated Fat 6g; Trans Fat 2g); Cholesterol 45mg; Sodium 480mg; Total Carbohydrate 72g (Dietary Fiber 2g; Sugars 45g); Protein 8g  % Daily Value: Vitamin A 4%; Vitamin C 0%; Calcium 6%; Iron 10%  Exchanges: 2 Starch, 3 Other Carbohydrate, 3 Fat  Carbohydrate Choices: 5

4 cups oats

3 cups Golden Grahams® cereal

3 cups Fiber One® cereal

1 cup chopped walnuts

1 cup sliced almonds

1 cup sunflower nuts

1 cup packed brown sugar

½ cup canola or vegetable oil

½ cup honey

½ cup water

½ teaspoon vanilla

½ teaspoon almond extract

# great day granola

**32 servings (½ cup each)**   |   Prep Time: **15 minutes**   |   Start to Finish: **2 hours 15 minutes**

1  Heat oven to 250°F. Spray 2 (15 × 10-inch) pans with sides with cooking spray. In very large bowl, mix oats, both cereals, the walnuts, almonds and sunflower nuts.

2  In 2-quart saucepan, cook brown sugar, oil, honey and water over medium-high heat 3 to 5 minutes, stirring constantly, until brown sugar is melted. Remove from heat. Stir in vanilla and almond extract. Pour over cereal mixture; stir until well coated. Spread mixture evenly in pans.

3  Bake 1 hour, rearranging pans once halfway through baking. Cool completely in pan, about 1 hour. Break into pieces. Store in tightly covered container. Serve as breakfast cereal, snack or as topping for ice cream, yogurt or fresh fruit.

High Altitude (3,500–6,500 ft): No change.

1 Serving: Calories 220 (Calories from Fat 90); Total Fat 10g (Saturated Fat 1g; Trans Fat 0g); Cholesterol 0mg; Sodium 65mg; Total Carbohydrate 27g (Dietary Fiber 5g; Sugars 13g); Protein 4g % Daily Value: Vitamin A 0%; Vitamin C 0%; Calcium 6%; Iron 15% Exchanges: 1 Starch, 1 Other Carbohydrate, 2 Fat Carbohydrate Choices: 2

Anita F. Hunter  |  Stilwell, KS

**Anita F. Hunter**'s three daughters "just loved" their grandmother's homemade granola. After preparing a few batches herself, she decided to adapt the recipe. This granola is now a family breakfast favorite. Each batch disappears quickly since it doubles as a snack and a topping. Anita remembers when her mother first tasted this recipe. "She turned, mouth still full, and said, 'Anita, this is a winner.'"

**Angela Buchanan** of Boulder, Colorado, won $10,000 and a new oven for her Cuban-Style Sandwiches with Green Chile au Jus (page 46).

Cuban-Style Sandwiches with Green Chile au Jus

# dinner made easy™

Bring on dinner with these easy-to-make main dish recipes for busy weeknights, including recipes that either can be prepared in 15 minutes or less—not including cooking, baking or cooling time—or can be completely prepared and ready to serve in 30 minutes.

## What's for Dinner?

Enchiladas lead that pack as a food, form and flavor for family dinners. The "Enchilada" name was given to recipes using a variety of fillings, including chicken, shrimp and spinach.

Calling the Internal Revenue Service—consider renaming April 15th Mexican Meatloaf Day! Several versions of this dish all arrived at the contest's judging agency on that date.

Pizza, a long-time favorite among home cooks, appeared with even more innovative toppings this year. Among the most creative were gravy and vegetables, green beans with almonds and roast beef topped with blue cheese. One cook even submitted a recipe for Spinach and Beets Pizza!

1 package (17 oz) refrigerated fully cooked pork roast au jus

1 can (13.2 oz) refrigerated country Italian loaf with pure olive oil

1 teaspoon ground cumin

2 teaspoons minced garlic in water (from a jar)

¼ lb thinly sliced cooked honey ham

4 slices (1 oz each) pepper Jack cheese

1 cup beef broth

1 can (4.5 oz) chopped green chiles

# cuban-style sandwiches with green chile au jus

**4 servings** (½ sandwich and ½ cup juice each)  |  Prep Time: **15 minutes**  |  Start to Finish: **45 minutes**

1 Heat oven to 350°F. Spray cookie sheet or 15 × 10 × 1-inch pan with cooking spray. Drain juice from pork roast into blender; set aside. Shred or chop pork into bite-size pieces; set aside.

2 Unroll dough into 1 large (about 14 × 9-inch) rectangle. With kitchen scissors or sharp knife, cut dough crosswise making 2 (9 × 7-inch) rectangles. Sprinkle each dough rectangle with ½ teaspoon cumin and 1 teaspoon garlic. Place half of ham and half of cheese in 3-inch-wide strip lengthwise down center of each dough rectangle. Divide pork evenly over cheese.

3 Bring long sides of dough up over filling to meet in center; pinch seam to seal. Pinch ends to seal. With pancake turner, place seam side down on cookie sheet or 15 × 10 × 1-inch pan. Cut 3 diagonal slashes in top of each sandwich.

4 Bake 25 to 30 minutes or until golden brown. Remove from cookie sheet; place on wire rack. Cool 5 minutes. Meanwhile, pour broth and undrained green chiles into blender with juice from pork; blend on medium-high speed 15 to 30 seconds or until smooth. Pour juice mixture into 2-cup microwavable measuring cup.

5 To serve, microwave juice mixture on High 2 to 3 minutes or until hot; divide mixture into 4 (6- or 8-oz) ramekins or cups. Cut each sandwich diagonally in half. Serve sandwiches with juice mixture for dipping.

High Altitude (3,500–6,500 ft): Bake 27 to 32 minutes.

1 Serving: Calories 620 (Calories from Fat 220); Total Fat 24g (Saturated Fat 9g; Trans Fat 0g); Cholesterol 140mg; Sodium 1720mg; Total Carbohydrate 45g (Dietary Fiber 0g; Sugars 5g); Protein 56g  % Daily Value: Vitamin A 6%; Vitamin C 6%; Calcium 20%; Iron 25% Exchanges: 3 Starch, 7 Lean Meat Carbohydrate Choices: 3

Angela Buchanan  |  Boulder, CO

**Angela Buchanan** may be a terrible singer, but she can whistle classical music, a talent she inherited from her father, who whistled classical music in the kitchen when she was growing up. This college teacher and her husband regularly work late and rely on quick, easy and tasty recipes like these sandwiches. Angela said her recipe is simple enough that even kids could help make it, and "everyone likes to dip a sandwich."

1 bag (19 oz) frozen roasted potatoes with garlic and herb sauce

1 cup diced fresh mozzarella cheese (6 oz)

⅓ cup sun-dried tomatoes in oil, drained, cut into strips

2 to 3 teaspoons chopped fresh rosemary

1 can (15 oz) cannellini (white kidney) beans, drained, rinsed

1 package (6 oz) refrigerated grilled chicken breast strips, heated in microwave as directed on package, coarsely chopped

⅓ cup basil pesto

2 teaspoons fresh lemon juice

Salt and pepper, if desired

3 cups mixed baby salad greens

¼ cup pine nuts, toasted*

*To toast pine nuts, place in single layer on cookie sheet; bake at 350°F 8 minutes, stirring once, until golden brown.

Karen Tedesco
Webster Groves, MO

"I love rustic, Mediterranean-style food," said **Karen Tedesco**. This busy mother also loves spending time with her two children. Her warm dinner salad is a great solution for a weeknight supper. Karen began to think about cooking during college, when she worked as a server at a small gourmet restaurant.

# tuscan roasted potato-chicken salad

**4 servings (1½ cups each)** | Prep Time: **30 minutes** | Start to Finish: **30 minutes**

1 In 2-quart microwavable bowl or casserole, microwave frozen potatoes and sauce chips, covered, on High 9 to 13 minutes, stirring once halfway through microwaving, until potatoes are tender. Stir potatoes to mix with sauce. Pour potato mixture into large bowl.

2 Stir in cheese, tomatoes, rosemary, beans and warm chicken. Add pesto and lemon juice; gently toss to coat. Season to taste with salt and pepper.

3 Arrange salad greens on large serving platter. Spoon potato salad over lettuce; sprinkle with pine nuts. Serve warm or at room temperature.

High Altitude (3,500–6,500 ft): No change.

1 Serving: Calories 610 (Calories from Fat 270); Total Fat 30g (Saturated Fat 10g; Trans Fat 1g); Cholesterol 55mg; Sodium 1290mg; Total Carbohydrate 48g (Dietary Fiber 10g; Sugars 4g); Protein 36g **% Daily Value:** Vitamin A 50%; Vitamin C 35%; Calcium 50%; Iron 30% **Exchanges:** 3 Starch, 1 Vegetable, 3½ Lean Meat, 3½ Fat **Carbohydrate Choices:** 3

1 can (10.1 oz) large refrigerated crescent dinner rolls

2 cups plain chicken salad for sandwiches (from deli)

¼ cup seedless green grapes, cut into quarters

¼ cup chopped fresh pineapple or drained canned pineapple tidbits

¼ cup chopped red apple

¼ cup drained canned mandarin orange segments

1 tablespoon packed brown sugar

4 roasted almond crunchy granola bars (2 pouches from 8.9-oz box), crushed (¾ cup)*

½ cup salad dressing or mayonnaise

*To easily crush granola bars, do not unwrap; use rolling pin to crush bars.

Jeremy Hodges I Pelham, AL

**Jeremy Hodges** admitted that, although his knowledge of cooking is limited, his knowledge of food isn't. "I like to eat," he explained. "As a college student, especially as a 20-year-old male, I know what tastes good and what I would actually be willing to make." Jeremy learned about the Bake-Off® Contest from the Internet. He brainstormed recipe ideas with his girlfriend and "kinda threw it together."

# granola–chicken salad sandwiches

**6 sandwiches** I Prep Time: **15 minutes** I Start to Finish: **25 minutes**

1 Heat oven to 350°F. Bake crescent rolls as directed on can. Remove from cookie sheet; cool on wire rack 5 minutes.

2 Meanwhile, in medium bowl, mix all remaining ingredients; refrigerate until needed.

3 Cut rolls horizontally in half. Fill with chicken salad mixture.

High Altitude (3,500–6,500 ft): No change.

1 Sandwich: Calories 490 (Calories from Fat 270); Total Fat 30g (Saturated Fat 6g; Trans Fat 2.5g); Cholesterol 40mg; Sodium 700mg; Total Carbohydrate 42g (Dietary Fiber 2g; Sugars 18g); Protein 13g  % Daily Value: Vitamin A 6%; Vitamin C 15%; Calcium 2%; Iron 10%  Exchanges: 2 Starch, ½ Fruit, ½ Other Carbohydrate, 1 Lean Meat, 5 Fat Carbohydrate Choices: 3

3 cups cubed cooked chicken (about 1 lb)

½ cup finely chopped, peeled jicama

½ cup finely chopped celery

½ cup chopped cashews

⅓ cup mayonnaise or salad dressing

2 teaspoons Dijon mustard

1 teaspoon curry powder

1 container (6 oz) lemon burst low-fat yogurt

Salt and pepper, if desired

1 can (16.3 oz) large refrigerated butter flavor flaky biscuits

4 cups mixed salad greens

# curried chicken salad waffle sandwiches

**4 sandwiches** | Prep Time: **30 minutes** | Start to Finish: **30 minutes**

1 In large bowl, mix chicken, jicama, celery and cashews. In small bowl, mix mayonnaise, mustard, curry powder and yogurt. Pour mayonnaise mixture over chicken mixture; gently toss to coat. Add salt and pepper to taste.

2 Heat Belgian or regular waffle maker (to make 2 or 4 waffle sections at a time). Separate dough into 8 biscuits; press or roll each into 4-inch round. Depending on size of waffle maker, place 2 to 4 biscuit rounds at a time in hot waffle maker. Bake 2 minutes or until golden brown. Cool 1 to 2 minutes.

3 Spoon and spread 1 cup chicken mixture onto each of 4 waffles; top with remaining waffles. Cut sandwiches in half; place 2 halves on each individual plate. Serve with mixed salad greens.

High Altitude (3,500–6,500 ft): No change.

1 Sandwich: Calories 860 (Calories from Fat 440); Total Fat 48g (Saturated Fat 10g; Trans Fat 7g); Cholesterol 100mg; Sodium 1410mg; Total Carbohydrate 64g (Dietary Fiber 3g; Sugars 19g); Protein 43g  % Daily Value: Vitamin A 60%; Vitamin C 20%; Calcium 20%; Iron 30% Exchanges: 3 Starch, 1 Other Carbohydrate, 1 Vegetable, 4½ Lean Meat, 6 ½ Fat Carbohydrate Choices: 4

Corvilia Carrington Thykkuttathil | Renton, WA

**Corvilia Carrington Thykkuttathil** describes her easy-to-prepare recipe as multicultural. By including both mustard greens and fried chicken with jicama, curry and yogurt, "it mixes the flavors of Black comfort food with the spices of my husband's East Indian family." Corvilia's cooking was influenced by her mom and grandma, who taught her: "Taste everything twice before you serve it."

¼ cup olive oil

3 cloves garlic, finely chopped

¼ cup all-purpose flour

Salt and pepper, if desired

1 lb chicken breast cut for scaloppine by butcher (or 1 lb boneless skinless chicken breasts pounded to ⅛-inch thickness)

1 can (6 oz) sliced mushrooms broiled in butter, drained

½ cup Marsala (sweet) wine or apple juice

1 can (18.5 oz) ready-to-serve French onion soup

4 kaiser rolls

4 oz fontina cheese, sliced, shaved or grated

1 tablespoon parsley flakes, if desired

Kelly Madey | Quakertown, PA

**Kelly Madey** adapted Chicken Marsala to a bistro-style sandwich, added cheese and served sauce on the side for dipping. She presented it to her husband to determine its Bake-Off® worthiness. "He loved it," she said. Julia Child supplied her favorite cooking tip: "If you're afraid of butter, use cream."

# chicken marsala sandwiches

**4 servings (1 sandwich and 3 tablespoons sauce each)**  |  Prep Time: **30 minutes**  |  Start to Finish: **30 minutes**

1   In small microwavable bowl, mix oil and garlic. Microwave on High 1 minute; set aside. Place flour on plate; stir in salt and pepper. Coat chicken with flour, shaking off excess.

2   In 12-inch nonstick skillet (1½ inches deep), place 1 tablespoon of the heated oil without garlic pieces. Heat oil over medium-high heat 1 to 2 minutes or until hot but not smoking. Add chicken, cutting large pieces in half, if necessary, so all chicken fits in skillet; cook 4 to 6 minutes, turning once, until no longer pink in center and golden brown. Remove chicken from skillet; place on plate and cover to keep warm.

3   In same skillet, cook mushrooms over medium-high heat 1 minute, stirring occasionally, until thoroughly heated. Stir in wine and soup with heatproof rubber spatula or wooden spoon to scrape up brown bits from bottom of skillet. Cook 5 to 7 minutes, stirring occasionally, until thoroughly heated.

4   Meanwhile, set oven control to broil. Split rolls; place cut side up on large cookie sheet. Broil 6 to 8 inches from heat 1 to 2 minutes or until toasted and golden brown. Brush cut sides with remaining oil mixture with garlic pieces; top evenly with fontina cheese. Broil 30 to 60 seconds or until cheese is melted.

5   Return chicken to skillet. Reduce heat to medium-low; simmer uncovered 2 to 3 minutes, turning chicken occasionally, until chicken is coated with sauce. Divide chicken evenly among rolls. With slotted spoon, divide mushrooms and onions over chicken. Pour wine sauce into 4 (4-oz) ramekins or dipping bowls. Sprinkle parsley on individual plates; place sandwiches and ramekins of sauce for dipping on plates.

High Altitude (3,500–6,500 ft): No change.

1 Serving: Calories 580 (Calories from Fat 260); Total Fat 29g (Saturated Fat 9g; Trans Fat 1g); Cholesterol 105mg; Sodium 1200mg; Total Carbohydrate 41g (Dietary Fiber 2g; Sugars 4g); Protein 39g  % Daily Value: Vitamin A 6%; Vitamin C 0%; Calcium 25%; Iron 20%  Exchanges: 2½ Starch, 4½ Lean Meat, 3 Fat  Carbohydrate Choices: 3

½ cup mayonnaise or salad dressing

¼ cup finely chopped English (seedless) cucumber

1½ to 3½ teaspoons Spanish smoked sweet paprika*

½ teaspoon freshly cracked black pepper

2 tablespoons honey

2 teaspoons olive oil

1½ lb chicken breast strips for stir-fry or 1½ lb boneless skinless chicken breasts, cut into thin bite-size strips

1 cup chunky-style salsa

1 package (11.5 oz) flour tortillas for burritos, 8 inch (8 tortillas)

8 leaves Bibb lettuce

*Spanish smoked sweet paprika can be purchased in a can or jar. Hungarian paprika can be substituted.

Patrice Hurd | Bemidji, MN

**Patrice Hurd's** grandmothers—one Finnish and one Slovenian—taught her many ethnic recipes. This retired hair salon owner's recipe is simple and quick to prepare, yet the smoky paprika imparts a depth of flavor that tastes like it's been simmering for hours. Patrice likes experimenting with herbs and spices and dreams of opening a spice store.

# sweet 'n smoky chicken wraps

8 wraps | Prep Time: **30 minutes** | Start to Finish: **30 minutes**

1 In small bowl, mix mayonnaise, cucumber, ½ teaspoon of the paprika, the pepper and I tablespoon of the honey; cover and refrigerate.

2 Heat 10-inch skillet over medium-high heat; add oil and heat until hot. Add chicken; cook 5 to 8 minutes, stirring frequently, until no longer pink in center. Stir in salsa, I teaspoon of the paprika and remaining tablespoon honey. Reduce heat to medium-low; simmer uncovered 5 minutes, stirring occasionally. For more paprika flavor, stir in up to 2 additional teaspoons paprika.

3 Heat tortillas as directed on package. Spread about I tablespoon mayonnaise mixture on each warm tortilla. Top each with I lettuce leaf and scant ½ cup chicken mixture. Fold bottom of each tortilla up over chicken mixture; roll sides in toward center. If necessary, secure with toothpicks; remove toothpicks before eating.

High Altitude (3,500–6,500 ft): No change.

1 Wrap: Calories 380 (Calories from Fat 170); Total Fat 19g (Saturated Fat 3.5g; Trans Fat 0g); Cholesterol 55mg; Sodium 670mg; Total Carbohydrate 30g (Dietary Fiber 0g; Sugars 6g); Protein 22g  % Daily Value: Vitamin A 20%; Vitamin C 0%; Calcium 8%; Iron 10%  **Exchanges:** 1½ Starch, ½ Other Carbohydrate, 2½ Very Lean Meat, 3½ Fat  Carbohydrate Choices: 2

1 lb lean (at least 80%) ground beef

1 box (9.2 oz) cheesy enchilada skillet-meal mix for hamburger

2 cups water

1 tablespoon red or white wine vinegar

½ to 1 teaspoon ground cinnamon

1 jar (16 oz) chunky-style salsa

3 tablespoons milk

½ cup raisins

½ cup slivered almonds

1 can (2.25 oz) sliced ripe olives, drained

1 package (11.5 oz) flour tortillas for burritos, 8 inch (8 tortillas), heated

Lime wedges, if desired

Fresh cilantro sprigs, if desired

# picadillo wraps

**8 wraps**  |  Prep Time: **30 minutes**  |  Start to Finish: **30 minutes**

1  In 12-inch skillet, cook ground beef over medium-high heat, stirring frequently, until thoroughly cooked; drain and return to skillet. Stir in uncooked Rice and Seasoning Mix, water, vinegar, cinnamon and salsa. Heat to boiling. Reduce heat to medium-low; cover and simmer 10 to 12 minutes, stirring occasionally, until rice is tender.

2  Meanwhile, in small bowl, stir milk and Topping Mix 30 seconds until blended; set aside.

3  Stir raisins, almonds and olives into beef mixture. Spoon about ¾ cup mixture down center of each warm tortilla; roll up. Serve wraps drizzled with topping; garnish plates with lime wedges and cilantro sprigs.

High Altitude (3,500–6,500 ft): Increase water to 2¼ cups. In step 1, simmer 12 to 14 minutes.

1 Wrap: Calories 470 (Calories from Fat 160); Total Fat 18g (Saturated Fat 4.5g; Trans Fat 1g); Cholesterol 35mg; Sodium 1260mg; Total Carbohydrate 59g (Dietary Fiber 2g; Sugars 10g); Protein 18g  % Daily Value: Vitamin A 8%; Vitamin C 0%; Calcium 15%; Iron 20%  Exchanges: 3 Starch, 1 Other Carbohydrate, 1½ Medium-Fat Meat, 1½ Fat Carbohydrate Choices: 4

Carol McLaughlin  |  Omaha, NE

When **Carol McLaughlin**'s mother started collecting cookbooks, Carol did, too. Now their respective collections number in the hundreds, and they talk about downsizing their treasured tomes. "But we can't bring ourselves to part with many," admits Carol. While considering ideas for the Bake-Off® Contest, she hit upon an idea to use Hamburger Helper® dinner mix as a picadillo base, then researched recipes online to learn about ingredients and spices her recipe would need for an authentic taste.

## Wraps

1 box (9 oz) frozen spinach

2 cups original flavor horn-shaped corn snacks

¼ cup butter, melted

1 can (8 oz) refrigerated crescent dinner rolls

16 thin slices cooked ham or turkey (about ½ lb)

4 sticks (1 oz each) string cheese

**Dipping Sauce, if desired**

⅓ cup mayonnaise or salad dressing

⅓ cup Dijon mustard

⅓ cup honey

Bobbie Keefer | Byers, CO

While her friends yearned to be in the Miss America competition, a young **Bobbie Keefer** dreamed of reaching the Bake-Off® Contest. And there she was, thanks to her culinary creativity and these wraps. "Each wrap looks like a gourmet sandwich," said Bobbie, "yet it's so easy to prepare—no slicing or dicing."

# crispy deli wraps

**4 wraps** | Prep Time: **15 minutes** | Start to Finish: **45 minutes**

1 Heat oven to 375°F. Line large cookie sheet with cooking parchment paper. Remove frozen spinach from pouch; place in colander. Rinse with warm water until thawed; drain well. Squeeze spinach dry with paper towel; divide evenly into 4 portions. Set aside.

2 Meanwhile, place corn snacks in resealable food-storage plastic bag; seal bag. With rolling pin, finely crush snacks; pour into shallow dish or pie plate. In another shallow dish or pie plate, place melted butter; set aside. Unroll dough; separate into 4 rectangles. Press each into 6 × 4-inch rectangle, firmly pressing perforations to seal.

3 Arrange ham in 4 stacks with 4 slices each. Top each stack with 1 portion of spinach, spreading spinach evenly over ham. Place 1 stick of cheese on one short side of spinach-topped ham. Roll up each stack.

4 Place 1 filled ham roll on one long side of each dough rectangle. Fold sides of dough up over ham roll and roll to opposite long side; press edge and ends to seal and completely cover ham roll. Roll each in butter, then in crushed corn snacks to coat; place seam side down on cookie sheet.

5 Bake 20 to 28 minutes or until deep golden brown. Meanwhile, in small bowl, mix all sauce ingredients with wire whisk. Serve warm wraps with sauce for dipping.

High Altitude (3,500–6,500 ft): Bake 24 to 28 minutes.

1 Wrap: Calories 560 (Calories from Fat 330); Total Fat 36g (Saturated Fat 19g; Trans Fat 4g); Cholesterol 75mg; Sodium 1520mg; Total Carbohydrate 32g (Dietary Fiber 2g; Sugars 5g); Protein 26g % Daily Value: Vitamin A 110%; Vitamin C 0%; Calcium 30%; Iron 20% Exchanges: 2 Starch, 3 Medium-Fat Meat, 4 Fat Carbohydrate Choices: 2

1 box (9 oz) frozen spinach

½ cup reduced-fat sour cream

1 tablespoon chopped fresh basil

1 tablespoon sun-dried tomato bits or chopped sun-dried tomatoes in oil

⅛ teaspoon salt

½ teaspoon lemon juice

1 clove garlic, finely chopped

8 flour tortillas for soft tacos and fajitas, 6 inch (from 10.5-oz package)

½ lb sliced cooked ham

1 jar (12 oz) sliced roasted red bell peppers in water, drained (about 1¼ cups)

8 oz sliced provolone cheese

# ham and spinach melts

**4 servings**  |  Prep Time: **20 minutes**  |  Start to Finish: **20 minutes**

1  Remove spinach from pouch; place in colander. Rinse with warm water until thawed; drain well. Squeeze spinach dry with paper towel. Meanwhile, in small bowl, mix sour cream, basil, tomatoes, salt, lemon juice and garlic.

2  On each tortilla, spread 1 tablespoon sour cream mixture. Top 4 tortillas evenly with ham, roasted peppers, spinach and cheese. Cover with remaining tortillas, sour cream mixture down.

3  Spray griddle or 12-inch skillet with cooking spray; heat over medium heat. Cook 2 sandwiches at a time 2 to 3 minutes on each side or until golden brown and thoroughly heated. Cut each sandwich in half to serve. Serve with your favorite soup or salad, if desired.

High Altitude (3,500–6,500 ft): No change.

1 Serving: Calories 520 (Calories from Fat 240); Total Fat 27g (Saturated Fat 14g; Trans Fat 0g); Cholesterol 80mg; Sodium 1680mg; Total Carbohydrate 36g (Dietary Fiber 2g; Sugars 8g); Protein 33g  % Daily Value: Vitamin A 180%; Vitamin C 80%; Calcium 60%; Iron 20%  Exchanges: 2 Starch, ½ Other Carbohydrate, 4 Medium-Fat Meat, 1 Fat Carbohydrate Choices: 2½

Anita L. Hunter  |  Newark, DE

When grilled-cheese lover **Anita L. Hunter** created these melts, she served her quick and delicious new recipe to her mother, who "loved it." In spite of her proficiency in the kitchen, she says she can't seem to properly roast a turkey, so Thanksgivings are always "an adventure. It's so bad my mom has threatened to contact the TV show *Food 911*," admitted Anita.

1 box (9 oz) frozen broccoli, carrots and
cauliflower in teriyaki sauce

1 green onion, coarsely chopped
(1 tablespoon)

1 lb lean ground pork

½ cup panko bread crumbs

1 teaspoon ground ginger

¼ cup mayonnaise or salad dressing

1 tablespoon teriyaki sauce

1 container (6 oz) orange crème or mandarin
orange low-fat yogurt

4 whole wheat or multi-grain burger buns
(4 to 5 inch), split, toasted

16 thin slices cucumber

# teriyaki veggie-pork burgers

**4 sandwiches** | Prep Time: **30 minutes** | Start to Finish: **30 minutes**

1 In food processor, place frozen teriyaki vegetables and onion; process
with on-and-off motions until finely chopped. Place in large bowl. Stir in
ground pork, bread crumbs and ginger until well blended. Shape mixture
into 4 patties, about 5 inches in diameter and ½ inch thick.

2 Spray 12-inch skillet with cooking spray; heat over medium heat. Add
patties; cover and cook 10 to 12 minutes, turning once, until browned and
meat thermometer inserted in center of patties reads 160°F.

3 Meanwhile, in small bowl, mix mayonnaise, teriyaki sauce and yogurt with
wire whisk until well blended.

4 Spread mayonnaise mixture evenly on top and bottom halves of toasted
buns. Top bottom halves with patties and cucumber slices. Cover with top
halves of buns.

High Altitude (3,500–6,500 ft): Cook over medium-high heat.

1 Sandwich: Calories 560 (Calories from Fat 280); Total Fat 31g (Saturated Fat 9g; Trans Fat 1g); Cholesterol 80mg;
Sodium 840mg; Total Carbohydrate 40g (Dietary Fiber 5g; Sugars 15g); Protein 28g  % Daily Value: Vitamin A 25%;
Vitamin C 10%; Calcium 15%; Iron 15%  Exchanges: 1½ Starch, 1 Other Carbohydrate, 1 Vegetable, 3 Medium-Fat Meat,
3 Fat  Carbohydrate Choices: 2½

Lisa Huff | Birmingham, AL

"My family loves Asian
pork dumplings, so I
adapted the recipe into a
burger," said **Lisa Huff.**
Her grandmother
inspired her—albeit indirectly—to
enter the contest. After her
grandmother passed away, Lisa
leafed through her old cookbooks
and recipes and found blank entry
forms from early Bake-Off®
Contests. "It sparked my interest,"
she said, "and the next thing I knew,
I was a finalist!"

1 can (13.8 oz) refrigerated pizza crust

¾ cup regular or reduced-fat mayonnaise

1 teaspoon lime or lemon juice

1 can (4.5 oz) chopped green chiles, drained

1 can (15 oz) dark red or red kidney beans, well drained

1 cup shredded cooked chicken

1½ cups shredded Mexican cheese blend (6 oz)

2 tablespoons chopped fresh cilantro, if desired

# cheesy bean and chicken pizza

**6 servings**  |  Prep Time: **15 minutes**  |  Start to Finish: **30 minutes**

1  Heat oven to 425°F. Lightly grease 14-inch pizza pan with shortening or cooking spray. Unroll dough; place in pan. Starting at center, press out dough to edge of pan. Bake 8 to 10 minutes or just until crust begins to brown around edge.

2  Meanwhile, in small bowl, mix mayonnaise, lime juice and chiles.

3  Gently spread mayonnaise mixture over partially baked crust. Top with beans, chicken and cheese. Bake 10 to 14 minutes longer or until crust is golden brown. Sprinkle with cilantro before serving.

High Altitude (3,500–6,500 ft): No change.

1 Serving: Calories 590 (Calories from Fat 310); Total Fat 34g (Saturated Fat 10g; Trans Fat 0g); Cholesterol 60mg; Sodium 900mg; Total Carbohydrate 47g (Dietary Fiber 4g; Sugars 6g); Protein 24g  % Daily Value: Vitamin A 8%; Vitamin C 4%; Calcium 25%; Iron 20%  Exchanges: 3 Starch, 2 Medium-Fat Meat, 4½ Fat  Carbohydrate Choices: 3

Patrice Kavanagh  |  Easton, PA

"My kids love the burritos I make, so I improvised to make a pizza," said **Patrice Kavanagh**. She prepared her Bake-Off® entry for a family gathering and received compliments on her creation. She says this pizza has good flavor and is quick, simple and fun to prepare. Now she serves it as an easy weeknight meal.

1 can (19 oz) cannellini (white kidney) beans, drained, rinsed

1 can (14.5 oz) organic diced tomatoes with Italian-style herbs, drained

1 package (6 oz) refrigerated cooked Italian-style chicken breast strips, cut into 1-inch pieces

1 tablespoon balsamic vinegar

½ teaspoon salt

1 can (11 oz) refrigerated soft breadsticks

2 cups shredded 6-cheese Italian cheese blend (8 oz)

½ teaspoon dried basil leaves, crushed

1 tablespoon chopped fresh parsley, if desired

# chicken and white bean bruschetta bake

**4 servings (1½ cups each)** | Prep Time: **15 minutes** | Start to Finish: **45 minutes**

1 Heat oven to 375°F. Spray 13 × 9-inch (3-quart) glass baking dish with cooking spray. In large bowl, mix beans, tomatoes, chicken, vinegar and salt.

2 Unroll dough; separate into 12 breadsticks. Cut each breadstick into 4 equal pieces. Stir ¼ of breadstick pieces at a time into bean mixture. Stir in 1 cup of the cheese. Spoon into baking dish, gently smoothing top. Top evenly with remaining 1 cup cheese; sprinkle with basil.

3 Bake 25 to 30 minutes or until bubbly and top is golden brown. To serve, spoon into individual shallow soup bowls; sprinkle with parsley.

High Altitude (3,500–6,500 ft): No change.

1 Serving: Calories 630 (Calories from Fat 180); Total Fat 20g (Saturated Fat 10g; Trans Fat 1g); Cholesterol 80mg; Sodium 1880mg; Total Carbohydrate 73g (Dietary Fiber 8g; Sugars 10g); Protein 40g % Daily Value: Vitamin A 20%; Vitamin C 15%; Calcium 45%; Iron 40% Exchanges: 3½ Starch, 1 Other Carbohydrate, 1 Vegetable, 4 Very Lean Meat, 3 Fat Carbohydrate Choices: 5

Shannon Kohn | Simpsonville, SC

What **Shannon Kohn** loves about this recipe is that "one bowl, nine ingredients and one baking dish equals dinner." She created this tasty combination of tomatoes, chicken, cannellini beans and herbs for herself and her two children one evening when her husband couldn't be home for dinner. She says it also includes cheese—a must in her house!

2½ teaspoons olive oil

½ cup Italian style dry bread crumbs

½ lb bulk chorizo sausage

1 teaspoon minced garlic in water (from a jar) or finely chopped fresh garlic

2 cups chopped skinned deli rotisserie chicken (from 2- to 2½-lb chicken)

1 cup organic sun-dried tomato pasta sauce

½ cup reduced-fat (lite) coconut milk (from 14-oz can), stirred well to blend

1 teaspoon mild taco seasoning mix (from 1.25-oz package)

½ teaspoon salt, if desired

¼ teaspoon pepper

1 can (15 oz) cannellini (white kidney) beans, undrained

2 to 3 tablespoons finely chopped fresh cilantro

4 sprigs fresh cilantro

Deborah Biggs | Omaha, NE

The first time she heard of cassoulet, **Deborah Biggs** was shocked by the recipe, which called for 22 ingredients and took three days to make. Deborah decided to come up with a quick, convenient and equally delicious version. Hers offers a Latin flair with coconut milk, seasonings and chorizo. Deborah's mother taught her how to cook, but she also learned a lesson from her cat who "sampled" a cake—planned as a county fair entry—as it cooled on a table.

# quick caribbean cassoulet

**4 servings (1¼ cups each)** | Prep Time: **30 minutes** | Start to Finish: **30 minutes**

1 In 10-inch nonstick skillet, mix oil and bread crumbs. Cook over medium heat 3 to 5 minutes, stirring frequently, just until crumb mixture begins to brown. Place crumbs in bowl; set aside for topping.

2 In same skillet, cook chorizo over medium heat 5 to 8 minutes, stirring frequently, until thoroughly cooked and browned. Add garlic; cook and stir 1 minute. Drain drippings from skillet. Stir in chicken, pasta sauce, coconut milk, taco seasoning mix, salt, pepper and beans. Heat to boiling. Reduce heat to medium-low; simmer uncovered 6 to 10 minutes, stirring frequently, until slightly thickened.

3 Stir in chopped cilantro. Ladle cassoulet into individual bowls. Sprinkle about 2 tablespoons bread crumb mixture over each serving and garnish with cilantro sprig.

High Altitude (3,500–6,500 ft): No change.

1 Serving: Calories 640 (Calories from Fat 290); Total Fat 33g (Saturated Fat 12g; Trans Fat 0g); Cholesterol 110mg; Sodium 1820mg; Total Carbohydrate 42g (Dietary Fiber 8g; Sugars 5g); Protein 45g  % Daily Value: Vitamin A 15%; Vitamin C 4%; Calcium 15%; Iron 35%  Exchanges: 2 Starch, 1 Other Carbohydrate, 5½ Lean Meat, 3 Fat  Carbohydrate Choices: 3

3 cups water

1 to 2 teaspoons salt

1 can (14.75 oz) cream style sweet corn

¾ cup quick-cooking grits

½ cup finely chopped green onions
(8 medium)

2 oz cream cheese

¼ cup butter

1 large clove garlic, finely chopped

1½ lb uncooked deveined peeled large shrimp

1 teaspoon seafood seasoning (from
6-oz container)

1 teaspoon chipotle chiles in adobo sauce
(from 7-oz can), finely chopped

1 can (14.5 oz) organic fire-roasted diced
tomatoes, drained

Lillian Jagendorf | New York, NY

"Growing up in New York, I never tried grits until I married a Southerner," said **Lillian Jagendorf**. Then, while visiting Charleston, South Carolina, she tried shrimp with grits. That spurred her to devise her own recipe, which she served to her Kentucky-born husband. "He loved it and often requests it," Lillian said. Julia Child was her greatest cooking influence; as a girl, she and her family regularly watched the popular cooking show.

# smoky shrimp with creamy grits

**4 servings (2½ cups each)** | Prep Time: **30 minutes** | Start to Finish: **30 minutes**

1 In 3-quart saucepan, heat water, salt and corn to boiling. With wire whisk, gradually beat in grits. Return to boiling, beating constantly. Reduce heat to low; cover and simmer 5 to 7 minutes, stirring occasionally, until thickened. Remove from heat. Stir in onions and cream cheese until well combined. Cover; keep warm.

2 Meanwhile, in 10-inch heavy skillet, melt butter over medium-high heat. Add garlic; cook and stir about 2 minutes or until lightly browned. Add shrimp; cook and stir 4 to 6 minutes or just until shrimp are pink. Stir in seafood seasoning, chipotle chiles and tomatoes. Reduce heat to medium; simmer uncovered 2 to 3 minutes or until tomatoes are thoroughly heated.

3 Divide grits mixture evenly among individual large soup bowls; spoon shrimp mixture evenly over top.

High Altitude (3,500–6,500 ft): No change.

1 Serving: Calories 480 (Calories from Fat 170); Total Fat 19g (Saturated Fat 11g; Trans Fat 1g); Cholesterol 290mg; Sodium 1720mg; Total Carbohydrate 45g (Dietary Fiber 2g; Sugars 11g); Protein 32g % Daily Value: Vitamin A 30%; Vitamin C 20%; Calcium 10%; Iron 35% Exchanges: 2 Starch, 1 Other Carbohydrate, 3½ Very Lean Meat, 3½ Fat Carbohydrate Choices: 3

### Chowder

2 tablespoons extra-virgin olive oil

1 cup chopped white onions (2 medium)

¼ cup chopped fresh poblano chile (about ½ chile)

½ teaspoon freshly ground black pepper

¼ teaspoon salt

1½ cups organic frozen whole kernel sweet corn (from 16-oz bag)

1 can (14.5 oz) organic fire-roasted diced tomatoes

1 can (14 oz) fat-free chicken broth with 33% less sodium

½ cup half-and-half

### Pesto

1 cup firmly packed fresh cilantro

2 tablespoons freshly grated Parmesan cheese

2 tablespoons roasted salted hulled pumpkin seeds (pepitas)

⅛ teaspoon salt

¼ teaspoon freshly ground black pepper

2 tablespoons extra-virgin olive oil

Jennifer Mohn  |  Austin, TX

**Jennifer Mohn** spent a Sunday afternoon tinkering with ingredients and serving soup to her husband. He really liked this chowder. Jennifer likes that this soup is truly easy to prepare, and despite the short cooking time, it has terrific flavor and texture. And cleanup is a snap since the Mohns installed a second dishwasher in their kitchen. Says Jennifer, "Now I could never go back to washing pots and pans by hand!"

# roasted tomato-corn chowder with cilantro pesto

**4 servings (1⅓ cups chowder and 1 heaping tablespoon pesto each)**

| Prep Time: **15 minutes**  | Start to Finish: **30 minutes**

1 In 3-quart saucepan, heat 2 tablespoons oil over medium-high heat. Add onions and chile; sprinkle with ½ teaspoon pepper and ¼ teaspoon salt. Cook, stirring frequently, 5 minutes. Stir in frozen corn, tomatoes and broth. Heat to boiling over high heat, stirring occasionally. Reduce heat to low; cover and simmer 10 to 15 minutes.

2 Meanwhile, in small food processor, place all pesto ingredients except oil; process with on-and-off motions 2 or 3 times to mix. With processor running, slowly drizzle 2 tablespoons oil into mixture, processing about 30 seconds or until well blended. Set pesto aside.

3 In blender or with immersion blender, blend chowder in 2 batches, if necessary, about 30 to 60 seconds or until almost smooth. Stir in half-and-half. Heat just until warm.

4 Ladle chowder into individual bowls. Top each with 1 heaping tablespoon pesto to be swirled in before eating.

High Altitude (3,500–6,500 ft): No change.

**1 Serving:** Calories 320 (Calories from Fat 190); Total Fat 21g (Saturated Fat 5g; Trans Fat 0g); Cholesterol 15mg; Sodium 780mg; Total Carbohydrate 24g (Dietary Fiber 4g; Sugars 8g); Protein 9g  **% Daily Value:** Vitamin A 25%; Vitamin C 25%; Calcium 10%; Iron 15%  **Exchanges:** 1 Starch, ½ Other Carbohydrate, 1 Vegetable, ½ High-Fat Meat, 3 Fat  **Carbohydrate Choices:** 1½

Blackberry-Almond Bruschetta

Winner **Karen Mack** of Webster, New York, created a lower-calorie Blackberry-Almond Bruschetta (page 82) but took home a big fat prize—$10,000 and a new oven.

### Bean Cakes

1 can (15 oz) black beans, drained

1 egg, slightly beaten

1 cup unseasoned dry bread crumbs

2 tablespoons finely chopped red onion

1 teaspoon garlic powder

1 teaspoon ground cumin

¼ teaspoon salt, if desired

1 teaspoon lime juice

1 can (4.5 oz) chopped green chiles

### Cilantro-Lime Sour Cream

½ cup reduced-fat sour cream

1 tablespoon chopped fresh cilantro

¼ teaspoon granulated sugar

⅛ teaspoon salt

2 teaspoons lime juice

### Salad

1 tablespoon granulated sugar

⅛ teaspoon salt

¼ cup extra-virgin olive oil

2 tablespoons red wine vinegar

2 teaspoons finely chopped jalapeño chile
(from jar)

1 teaspoon jalapeño liquid (from jar)

1 bag (5 oz) spring or baby greens salad mix

### Garnish

Fresh sprigs of cilantro, if desired

Lisa Silcox | Abingdon, VA

**Lisa Silcox** wasn't betting on winning a spot in the Bake-Off® Contest. But she entered any way because, she explained, "I decided I had a better chance at winning than my husband does at playing the lottery." When told she was a finalist, Lisa was so jubilant that she broke into a "happy dance"—and then broke her toe. A physical therapist, Lisa snapped her toe back into place and continued her dance.

# black bean cake salad with cilantro-lime cream

**6 servings**  |  Prep Time: **35 minutes**  |  Start to Finish: **35 minutes**

1  Heat oven to 400°F. Spray cookie sheet with cooking spray. In medium bowl, mash beans with fork or pastry blender. Stir in egg, ¾ cup of the bread crumbs and remaining bean cake ingredients. Shape mixture into 6 patties, 3 inches in diameter and ½ inch thick. Sprinkle both sides of bean patties with remaining ¼ cup bread crumbs; place on cookie sheet.

2  Bake 10 minutes. Turn bean cakes over; bake 10 to 13 minutes longer or until bread crumbs begin to turn golden brown.

3  Meanwhile, in small bowl, mix all cilantro-lime sour cream ingredients; set aside. In large bowl, beat all salad ingredients except salad mix with wire whisk until well blended. Add salad mix; toss until coated.

4  To serve, arrange salad evenly on individual plates. Top each with bean cake and dollop of cilantro-lime sour cream. Garnish with cilantro sprigs.

High Altitude (3,500–6,500 ft): No change.

1 Serving: Calories 310 (Calories from Fat 120); Total Fat 14g (Saturated Fat 3.5g; Trans Fat 0g); Cholesterol 45mg; Sodium 600mg; Total Carbohydrate 35g (Dietary Fiber 5g; Sugars 7g); Protein 10g  % Daily Value: Vitamin A 25%; Vitamin C 15%; Calcium 10%; Iron 20%  Exchanges: 1½ Starch, ½ Other Carbohydrate, 1 Vegetable, ½ Lean Meat, 2½ Fat  Carbohydrate Choices: 2

2 cups ¾-inch pieces skinned lemon-pepper
  or regular deli rotisserie chicken breast
  (from 2- to 2½-lb chicken)

¼ cup mango chutney

½ teaspoon ground mustard

4 green onions, sliced (¼ cup)

1 container (6 oz) piña colada low-fat yogurt

1 can (8 oz) refrigerated reduced-fat
  crescent dinner rolls

½ teaspoon lemon-dill salt-free seasoning

¼ teaspoon coarse ground black pepper

4 medium green onions

4 teaspoons mango chutney

Susan Scarborough |
Fernandina Beach, FL

**Susan Scarborough** gets most of her recipe ideas from old classic recipes (especially Southern) and from her travel experiences. "These cannoli look like little exotic gifts," said Susan, "but they are really simple." She recalled when her French foreign exchange student was teaching her how to make a dish. He grabbed a giant box of kosher salt, presuming it was sugar, and dumped in a cup before she could stop him.

# chicken salad crescent cannoli

**4 servings** | Prep Time: **20 minutes** | Start to Finish: **45 minutes**

1  Heat oven to 350°F. In medium bowl, mix chicken, ¼ cup chutney, the mustard, sliced onions and yogurt with fork until well blended. Refrigerate until needed.

2  Cut 4 (12-inch) squares of heavy-duty foil. Place 1 foil square on work surface; fold into thirds to make a triple-thick 12 × 4-inch strip. Starting with one 4-inch end, roll foil strip into tube with 1¼-inch inside diameter. Repeat with remaining foil squares.

3  Unroll dough; separate into 4 rectangles, pressing perforations to seal. Place 1 foil tube on one short side of each rectangle; roll dough around tube. Place seam side down 2 inches apart on ungreased cookie sheet. Sprinkle each evenly with lemon-dill seasoning and pepper.

4  Bake 12 to 15 minutes or until golden brown. Remove from cookie sheet; place on wire rack. Cool 5 minutes. To remove foil from each crescent cannoli, grasp inside corner of foil and pull to uncoil foil from dough. Cool 5 minutes longer.

5  Fill each crescent cannoli with ½ cup chicken mixture; place on individual plate. Place any extra chicken mixture near open ends of each cannoli. To garnish, cut off white ends from 4 green onions; save for later use. Cut each green portion lengthwise into 2 strips; tie ends of each pair to form a knot. Place knot on top of each cannoli, tucking ends under sides. Spoon 1 teaspoon chutney onto plate at side of each cannoli.

High Altitude (3,500–6,500 ft): No change.

1 Serving: Calories 400 (Calories from Fat 130); Total Fat 15g (Saturated Fat 3.5g; Trans Fat 2g); Cholesterol 60mg; Sodium 840mg; Total Carbohydrate 41g (Dietary Fiber 2g; Sugars 18g); Protein 26g % Daily Value: Vitamin A 10%; Vitamin C 6%; Calcium 10%; Iron 15% Exchanges: 1½ Starch, 1 Other Carbohydrate, 3 Lean Meat, 1 Fat Carbohydrate Choices: 3

1 tablespoon extra-virgin olive oil

1½ lb uncooked chicken breast tenders (not breaded)

8 to 10 small to medium zucchini (2½ lb), peeled, thinly sliced (8 cups)

1 medium white onion, chopped (½ cup)

1 can (15.25 oz) whole kernel corn, undrained

1 can (14.5 oz) diced tomatoes with green pepper and onion, undrained

1 can (4.5 oz) chopped green chiles, undrained

1½ teaspoons garlic powder

½ teaspoon ground cumin

Salt and pepper, if desired

½ cup chopped fresh cilantro

# calabacita chicken stew

**6 servings (1⅔ cups each)** | Prep Time: **10 minutes** | Start to Finish: **50 minutes**

1 In 5- to 6-quart saucepan or Dutch oven, heat oil over medium heat. Add chicken; cover and cook 4 to 6 minutes, stirring occasionally, until no longer pink in center.

2 Stir in remaining ingredients except cilantro. Heat to boiling. Reduce heat to medium-low; cover and simmer about 20 minutes, stirring occasionally, until zucchini is tender.

3 Stir in cilantro; cook 3 minutes longer, stirring occasionally.

High Altitude (3,500–6,500 ft): No change.

1 Serving: Calories 270 (Calories from Fat 60); Total Fat 7g (Saturated Fat 1.5g; Trans Fat 0g); Cholesterol 70mg; Sodium 470mg; Total Carbohydrate 24g (Dietary Fiber 4g; Sugars 9g); Protein 28g  % Daily Value: Vitamin A 25%; Vitamin C 20%; Calcium 8%; Iron 15%  Exchanges: ½ Starch, ½ Other Carbohydrate, 2 Vegetable, 3 Very Lean Meat, 1 Fat  Carbohydrate Choices: 1½

Linda S. Brown | Dallas, TX

A fourth-generation Mexican-American, **Linda S. Brown** learned to cook by watching her mother, not following recipe cards. Her specialty is re-inventing the Mexican-American dishes she grew up with into heart-healthy meals. The origin of this stew, which "blends flavorful ingredients that warm the soul," probably goes back many generations.

1/4 cup chopped fresh cilantro or parsley

1/4 cup mojo criollo marinade (Spanish marinating sauce) or zesty Italian dressing

1/2 small red onion, cut into very thin strips

1/4 teaspoon kosher (coarse) salt

1/8 teaspoon cracked black pepper

1 can (15 oz) black beans, drained, rinsed

1 package (6 oz) refrigerated grilled chicken strips*

1 can (13.8 oz) refrigerated pizza crust

3/4 cup shredded Monterey Jack cheese (3 oz)

3/4 cup shredded mozzarella cheese (3 oz)

*One large boneless skinless chicken breast, cooked on the grill and cut into thin strips, can be used in place of the refrigerated grilled chicken strips.

Ginny Solomon | Brooksville, FL

The desire for a nutritious dinner, some leftover grilled chicken, and a "pizza-loving family" combined to inspire **Ginny Solomon** to create a leaner pizza with "a wow factor." It has since become a favorite lunch or dinner choice in her household. As a little girl in her grandmother's kitchen, she remembers stirring bouillon cubes into canned soup as though she'd created a masterpiece. Today, soups are still her specialty. "Don't be afraid to substitute ingredients," advised Ginny. "A recipe is just a guide."

# mojo black bean–chicken pizza

**8 servings**  |  Prep Time: **20 minutes**  |  Start to Finish: **30 minutes**

1  Heat oven to 400°F. In medium bowl, mix cilantro, marinade, onion, salt, pepper, beans and chicken. Let stand 10 to 15 minutes to marinate.

2  Meanwhile, lightly spray large cookie sheet with cooking spray. Unroll dough on cookie sheet; starting in center, press into 15 × 11-inch rectangle. Bake 8 to 12 minutes or until light golden brown.

3  Spread chicken mixture over partially baked crust to within 1/2 inch of edges. Sprinkle both cheeses over top. Bake 8 minutes longer or until cheese is melted and crust is golden brown around edges. Cut into 8 rectangles.

High Altitude (3,500–6,500 ft): No change.

1 Serving: Calories 290 (Calories from Fat 70); Total Fat 8g (Saturated Fat 4g; Trans Fat 0g); Cholesterol 30mg; Sodium 870mg; Total Carbohydrate 37g (Dietary Fiber 3g; Sugars 5g); Protein 18g  % Daily Value: Vitamin A 4%; Vitamin C 0%; Calcium 20%; Iron 15% Exchanges: 2 Starch, 1/2 Other Carbohydrate, 1 1/2 Medium-Fat Meat Carbohydrate Choices: 2 1/2

1¼ cups organic medium chipotle salsa

¼ cup orange marmalade

5 tablespoons lime juice

Salt and pepper, if desired

6 boneless skinless chicken breasts (1¾ lb)

¾ cup garlic-herb dry bread crumbs

¼ cup grated Parmesan cheese

2 tablespoons chopped fresh cilantro

2 cups organic frozen whole kernel sweet
corn (from 16-oz bag), thawed

1 bag (10 oz) organic frozen shelled
edamame, thawed

1 teaspoon ground cumin

Fresh cilantro sprigs, if desired

Rebecca R. Saulsbury | Lakeland, FL

"I'm always trying to figure
out ways to create fast,
easy and tasty meals," said
**Rebecca R. Saulsbury**, an
assistant professor of
English and co-director of a college
African-American studies program.
This chicken and succotash dinner
features comforting flavors and easy
preparation without the high fat and
calories of fried chicken.

# breaded chicken with edamame succotash

**6 servings**  |  Prep Time: **30 minutes**  |  Start to Finish: **1 hour 15 minutes**

1 In small bowl, mix ½ cup of the salsa, the marmalade and 4 tablespoons of the lime juice; season with salt and pepper. Pour into large resealable food-storage plastic bag. Add chicken; seal bag. Turn bag several times to coat chicken. Refrigerate 30 minutes.

2 Heat oven to 375°F. In another large resealable food-storage plastic bag, mix bread crumbs, cheese and chopped cilantro. Remove 1 chicken breast at a time from marinade; shake off excess marinade. Place in bag of bread crumbs; seal bag and shake to coat with crumb mixture. Place chicken on nonstick cookie sheet. Discard any remaining marinade and crumb mixture.

3 Bake uncovered 20 to 25 minutes, turning once, until juice of chicken is clear when center of thickest part is cut (170°F). Meanwhile, in 2-quart saucepan, place corn and edamame; add enough water to just cover vegetables. Heat to boiling over medium-high heat. Reduce heat to medium-low; cook uncovered 5 to 6 minutes or just until edamame is tender. Drain; stir in remaining ¾ cup salsa, the cumin and remaining tablespoon lime juice. Season to taste with salt and pepper. Cook over medium-low heat 1 to 3 minutes, stirring occasionally, until thoroughly heated.

4 Serve chicken with succotash; garnish with cilantro sprigs.

High Altitude (3,500–6,500 ft): Bake chicken uncovered 30 to 35 minutes.

1 **Serving:** Calories 360 (Calories from Fat 80); Total Fat 9g (Saturated Fat 2.5g; Trans Fat 0g); Cholesterol 85mg; Sodium 660mg; Total Carbohydrate 29g (Dietary Fiber 4g; Sugars 7g); Protein 40g  % **Daily Value:** Vitamin A 6%; Vitamin C 15%; Calcium 15%; Iron 20%  **Exchanges:** 1½ Starch, ½ Other Carbohydrate, 5 Very Lean Meat, 1 Fat **Carbohydrate Choices:** 2

1 can (16.3 oz) large refrigerated reduced-fat
buttermilk homestyle biscuits

1 egg yolk

¼ teaspoon water

1 tablespoon sesame seed

⅓ cup reduced-fat mayonnaise or
salad dressing

2 tablespoons finely chopped fresh cilantro

⅛ teaspoon salt

⅛ teaspoon pepper

⅛ teaspoon Cajun seasoning

1 can (4.5 oz) chopped green chiles

2 cans (6 oz each) albacore tuna in
water, drained

2 cups shredded reduced-fat Cheddar
cheese (8 oz)

Chopped tomato, if desired

Shredded lettuce, if desired

Cindy Gedling | Little Rock, AR

What was **Cindy Gedling**'s reaction when she learned she was a Bake-Off® finalist? "To say I was excited is an understatement . . . screams and shouts disrupted the entire office area, I breathlessly relayed the news, shook like a leaf and then danced for joy!" She developed the tuna portion of her recipe years ago as a party dip. The rest came later, when Cindy wanted the same taste of the tuna-melt sandwiches she enjoyed as a child but without all the calories and fat.

# grands!® tuna and green chile melt

**8 open-face sandwiches**  |  Prep Time: **25 minutes**  |  Start to Finish: **25 minutes**

1 Heat oven to 350°F. Spray large cookie sheet with cooking spray. Separate dough into 8 biscuits; place 2½ inches apart on cookie sheet. With bottom of flat 2-inch-diameter glass or with fingers, press biscuits into 3½-inch rounds with ¼-inch rim around outer edge.

2 In small bowl, beat egg yolk and water with fork until well blended. Brush over tops and sides of biscuits. Sprinkle each with sesame seed. Bake 13 to 17 minutes or until golden brown.

3 Meanwhile, in medium bowl, mix mayonnaise, cilantro, salt, pepper, Cajun seasoning and green chiles. Stir in tuna; set aside.

4 Set oven control to broil. Spoon about ¼ cup tuna mixture into indentation in each biscuit; sprinkle each with ¼ cup cheese. Broil 4 to 6 inches from heat 1 to 2 minutes or until cheese is melted. Carefully remove biscuits from cookie sheet. Garnish with tomato and lettuce.

High Altitude (3,500–6,500 ft): No change.

1 **Open-Face Sandwich:** Calories 310 (Calories from Fat 110); Total Fat 13g (Saturated Fat 4g; Trans Fat 2g); Cholesterol 45mg; Sodium 1150mg; Total Carbohydrate 27g (Dietary Fiber 0g; Sugars 5g); Protein 21g **% Daily Value:** Vitamin A 2%; Vitamin C 2%; Calcium 25%; Iron 15% **Exchanges:** 1½ Starch, ½ Other Carbohydrate, 2½ Very Lean Meat, 2 Fat **Carbohydrate Choices:** 2

2 teaspoons vegetable oil

1 large yellow onion, chopped (about 1 cup)

1 medium red bell pepper, chopped
  (about 1 cup)

1 can (20 oz) pineapple tidbits in juice,
  drained, ⅓ cup juice reserved

1 can (15 oz) black beans, drained, rinsed

1 can (4.5 oz) chopped green chiles

1 teaspoon salt

½ cup chopped fresh cilantro

3 cups shredded reduced-fat Cheddar
  cheese (12 oz)

1 can (10 oz) mild enchilada sauce

8 whole wheat flour tortillas (8 or 9 inch)

½ cup reduced-fat sour cream

8 teaspoons chopped fresh cilantro

# pineapple–black bean enchiladas

**8 servings**  |  Prep Time: **30 minutes**  |  Start to Finish: **1 hour 10 minutes**

1 Heat oven to 350°F. Spray 13 × 9-inch (3-quart) glass baking dish with cooking spray. In 12-inch nonstick skillet, heat oil over medium heat. Add onion and bell pepper; cook 4 to 5 minutes or until softened. Stir in pineapple, beans, green chiles and salt. Cook and stir until thoroughly heated. Remove skillet from heat. Stir in ½ cup cilantro and 2 cups of the cheese.

2 Spoon and spread 1 tablespoon enchilada sauce onto each tortilla. Spoon about ¾ cup vegetable mixture over sauce on each. Roll up tortillas; place seam side down in baking dish.

3 In small bowl, mix reserved ⅓ cup pineapple juice and remaining enchilada sauce; pour over entire surface of enchiladas in dish. Sprinkle with remaining 1 cup cheese. Spray sheet of foil large enough to cover baking dish with cooking spray; place sprayed side down over baking dish and seal tightly.

4 Bake 35 to 40 minutes, removing foil during last 5 to 10 minutes of baking, until cheese is melted and sauce is bubbly. Top each baked enchilada with 1 tablespoon sour cream and 1 teaspoon cilantro.

High Altitude (3,500–6,500 ft): Bake 40 to 45 minutes, removing foil during last 5 to 10 minutes of baking.

1 Serving: Calories 330 (Calories from Fat 70); Total Fat 7g (Saturated Fat 3g; Trans Fat 0g); Cholesterol 15mg; Sodium 1110mg; Total Carbohydrate 48g (Dietary Fiber 7g; Sugars 17g); Protein 19g  % Daily Value: Vitamin A 20%; Vitamin C 40%; Calcium 40%; Iron 15%  Exchanges: 2 Starch, 1 Other Carbohydrate, 2 Lean Meat  Carbohydrate Choices: 3

Mary Iovinelli Buescher |
Bloomington, MN

**Mary Iovinelli Buescher** developed this enchilada recipe for her best friend's bridal shower. She wanted to please her friend—a vegetarian—and satisfy guests accustomed to eating meat. Her recipe, which offers both sweet and spicy flavors, was a hit. Mary describes it as "an easy-to-make recipe with so much flavor you forget it is healthy."

1 lb boneless pork loin chops (¾ to
 1 inch thick)

Salt and pepper, if desired

1 cup organic frozen sliced peaches
 (from 10-oz bag), slightly thawed,
 coarsely chopped

1 cup organic medium chipotle salsa

3 tablespoons honey

3 tablespoons red wine vinegar

2 tablespoons finely chopped garlic (10 to
 12 medium cloves)

1 box (4.7 oz) taco shells (10 shells)

½ small red onion, thinly sliced

2½ cups chopped romaine lettuce

2 avocados, pitted, peeled and cut into
 10 wedges, if desired

2 limes, cut into 10 wedges

1 small bunch fresh cilantro, if desired

# peachy chipotle-pork tacos

**5 servings (2 tacos each)**  |  Prep Time: **30 minutes**  |  Start to Finish: **30 minutes**

1 Heat 12-inch nonstick skillet over medium-high heat. Sprinkle pork chops with salt and pepper; add to skillet. Cook 8 to 10 minutes, turning once, until meat thermometer inserted in center of chops reads 160°F. Remove from skillet; place on cutting board to cool slightly. Remove skillet from heat.

2 To same skillet, carefully add peaches, salsa, honey, vinegar and garlic. Cook over medium-high heat about 5 minutes, stirring constantly, until mixture is thickened. Cut pork into ½-inch pieces; stir into peach mixture. Meanwhile, heat taco shells as directed on box.

3 To serve, divide pork mixture evenly among warm taco shells. Top each with onion and lettuce. Garnish each with 1 avocado wedge; squeeze juice from 1 lime wedge over each and garnish with cilantro.

High Altitude (3,500–6,500 ft): No change.

1 Serving: Calories 360 (Calories from Fat 120); Total Fat 13g (Saturated Fat 3.5g; Trans Fat 2g); Cholesterol 55mg; Sodium 370mg; Total Carbohydrate 39g (Dietary Fiber 4g; Sugars 16g); Protein 23g  % Daily Value: Vitamin A 40%; Vitamin C 60%; Calcium 6%; Iron 10%  Exchanges: 1½ Starch, 1 Other Carbohydrate, 2½ Lean Meat, 1 Fat  Carbohydrate Choices: 2½

Natalie Hval  |  Portland, OR

**Natalie Hval** once made hot-and-sour soup and used baking soda instead of cornstarch. (The jar was labeled incorrectly.) Between the vinegar and soda, "it became a fizzing science experiment," she said. No matter, Natalie's father taught her to persevere, to have fun and not to be afraid to experiment in the kitchen. Her taco recipe "zings the taste buds" with a combination of sweet, tart, salty and hot.

4 eggs

2 bags (1 lb each) frozen cauliflower florets

1 bag (10 oz) organic frozen peas and carrots

1¾ cups reduced-fat mayonnaise or
salad dressing

1 teaspoon sugar

1 teaspoon salt

¼ teaspoon pepper

¼ teaspoon paprika

1 tablespoon cider vinegar

1 teaspoon yellow mustard

1 cup chopped celery (2½ stalks)

⅔ cup chopped onion (about 1 medium)

Lori Holtsclaw | Rochester Hills, MI

**Lori Holtsclaw** mixed together leftover cauliflower and leftover potato salad for lunch and originated her Bake-Off® recipe. "You really won't know it's not potato salad," she said. There are no potatoes to peel; cauliflower stars in this tasty salad. Lori didn't always know her way around the kitchen so well. At her husband's suggestion, she bought a "really big" cookbook and followed the recipes.

# you won't know it's not potato salad

**16 servings (½ cup each)**   |   Prep Time: **40 minutes**   |   Start to Finish: **2 hours 5 minutes**

1 In 2-quart saucepan, place eggs in single layer; add enough cold water to cover eggs by 1 inch. Cover; heat to boiling. Remove from heat; let stand covered 15 minutes. Drain eggs. Immediately run cold water over eggs until completely cooled. Peel and chop eggs.

2 Meanwhile, in large (4-quart) microwavable bowl, place frozen cauliflower and frozen peas and carrots; cover with microwavable waxed paper. Microwave on High 20 to 25 minutes, stirring once halfway through microwaving. Drain vegetables in colander; rinse with cold water to cool. Place colander over same large bowl; refrigerate at least 30 minutes or until cooled.

3 In small bowl, mix mayonnaise, sugar, salt, pepper, ⅛ teaspoon of the paprika, the vinegar and mustard; set aside.

4 Remove vegetables from refrigerator; discard any liquid in bowl. Pat drained vegetables dry with paper towels; chop any large cauliflower pieces into ¾-inch chunks to resemble chopped potatoes. Place cauliflower, peas and carrots in same bowl. Add celery, onion and chopped eggs.

5 Pour mayonnaise mixture over salad; stir until vegetables and eggs are well coated. Sprinkle remaining ⅛ teaspoon paprika over salad. If desired, cover and refrigerate at least 1 hour or until well chilled before serving.

High Altitude (3,500–6,500 ft): In step 1, after heating water with eggs to boiling, boil gently 5 minutes. Remove from heat; cover and let stand 15 minutes.

1 Serving: Calories 130 (Calories from Fat 90); Total Fat 10g (Saturated Fat 2g; Trans Fat 0g); Cholesterol 60mg; Sodium 370mg; Total Carbohydrate 7g (Dietary Fiber 2g; Sugars 3g); Protein 3g  % Daily Value: Vitamin A 35%; Vitamin C 15%; Calcium 2%; Iron 4% Exchanges: 1 Vegetable, 2 Fat Carbohydrate Choices: ½

2 cups Cinnamon Toast Crunch® cereal

1 cup Fiber One® cereal

1½ cups flaked coconut

1 cup pecan halves

1 cup blanched whole almonds

½ cup sunflower nuts

½ cup wheat germ

½ cup ground flax seed

1 teaspoon salt

1 teaspoon ground cinnamon

¼ cup vegetable oil

1 can (14 oz) fat-free sweetened condensed milk (not evaporated)

1 cup chopped dried apricots

1 cup banana chips

1 cup sweetened dried cranberries

½ cup dried cherries

½ cup golden raisins

# cinnamon-fruit snack mix

**32 servings (½ cup each)** | Prep Time: **20 minutes** | Start to Finish: **1 hour 50 minutes**

1 Heat oven to 300°F. Spray 15 × 10 × 1-inch pan with cooking spray. In large bowl, place both cereals, coconut, pecans, almonds, sunflower nuts, wheat germ, flax seed, salt and cinnamon; mix well. In small bowl, mix oil and condensed milk. Pour over cereal mixture; toss until well coated. Spread evenly in pan.

2 Bake 50 to 60 minutes, stirring every 15 minutes to break up any large clumps, until light golden brown. Cool 30 minutes.

3 In large bowl, mix cereal mixture, apricots, banana chips, cranberries, cherries and raisins. Store in tightly covered container.

High Altitude (3,500–6,500 ft): No change.

1 Serving: Calories 220 (Calories from Fat 100); Total Fat 11g (Saturated Fat 3g; Trans Fat 0g); Cholesterol 0mg; Sodium 125mg; Total Carbohydrate 27g (Dietary Fiber 4g; Sugars 19g); Protein 4g  % Daily Value: Vitamin A 6%; Vitamin C 0%; Calcium 8%; Iron 10%  Exchanges: 1 Starch, 1 Other Carbohydrate, 2 Fat  Carbohydrate Choices: 2

Rebecca Nurse | Waterford, PA

"It had been 'one of those days,'" said **Rebecca Nurse**, remembering when she got the call telling her she was a Bake-Off® finalist. She found this hilarious. "It just seemed funny to me that something so extraordinary could happen on such an ordinary day." According to Rebecca, this snack mix is a scrumptious blend of ingredients that everyone (including children) enjoys.

**Crust**

1 refrigerated pie crust (from 15-oz box),
softened as directed on box

**Filling**

1 cup skim (fat-free) milk

1 package unflavored gelatin

¼ cup sugar blend for baking

1½ cups part-skim ricotta cheese (12 oz)

½ teaspoon vanilla

1 cup frozen (thawed) fat-free
whipped topping

2 containers (6 oz each) very vanilla
fat-free yogurt

**Strawberry Sauce**

¼ cup sugar blend for baking

1 tablespoon cornstarch

1 bag (10 oz) organic frozen
strawberries, thawed

1 tablespoon lemon juice

Jean Gottfried |
Upper Sandusky, OH

I have never been a big
milk drinker, admitted
**Jean Gottfried**. But
believing that adding
dairy would improve her
diet, she began experimenting with
different recipes to vary the ways to
add it in. Her husband acted as "first
recipe critic and guinea pig." He is
diabetic, so watching carbohydrates
is important for Jean, but so is
pleasing his taste buds. She tried
several flavor combinations before
finding one he liked.

# italian cream pie with strawberry sauce

**12 servings** | Prep Time: **50 minutes** | Start to Finish: **3 hours 50 minutes**

1 Heat oven to 450°F. Unroll pie crust; place in 8- or 9-inch springform pan, pressing crust up side of pan to top edge. (Do not overwork or let crust get too warm.) Prick bottom and side of crust with fork. Bake 9 to 11 minutes or until lightly browned. Cool completely, about 30 minutes.

2 Meanwhile, in 1-quart saucepan, place ½ cup of the milk. Sprinkle gelatin over milk; let stand 5 minutes to soften. Stir in remaining ½ cup milk and ¼ cup sugar blend. Cook on low heat, stirring frequently, until gelatin is completely dissolved (do not boil). Pour milk mixture into blender. Add ricotta cheese and vanilla; cover and blend until pureed. Pour into large bowl; stir in whipped topping and yogurt.

3 Remove side of pan; remove crust from pan and place crust on serving plate. To create collar for crust, wrap piece of string around outside of crust to measure; cut sheet of waxed paper length of string plus 3 inches. Fold waxed paper in half lengthwise; fold in half again. Wrap around outside of crust; staple collar together to secure around crust. Pour filling into cooled baked crust. Refrigerate until set, about 2 to 3 hours.

4 In 1½-quart saucepan, mix ¼ cup sugar blend and the cornstarch. Stir in thawed strawberries. Cook over medium heat, stirring constantly, until slightly thickened. Remove from heat. Stir in lemon juice. Refrigerate until serving time.

5 To serve, remove waxed paper collar. Cut into wedges; place on individual dessert plates. Top servings with strawberry sauce. Store dessert and sauce in refrigerator.

High Altitude (3,500–6,500 ft): No change.

1 Serving: Calories 210 (Calories from Fat 70); Total Fat 7g (Saturated Fat 3.5g; Trans Fat 0g); Cholesterol 15mg; Sodium 140mg; Total Carbohydrate 29g (Dietary Fiber 0g; Sugars 17g); Protein 6g  % Daily Value: Vitamin A 6%; Vitamin C 10%; Calcium 15%; Iron 0% Exchanges: 1 Starch, 1 Other Carbohydrate, 1½ Fat Carbohydrate Choices: 2

1 bag (12 oz) dark chocolate chips (2 cups)

1 container (6 oz) raspberry low-fat yogurt

6 roasted almond crunchy granola bars
(3 pouches from 8.9-oz box), finely
crushed (heaping 1 cup)*

1 cup egg whites (about 7)

2 tablespoons plus 1 teaspoon fat-free
half-and-half

2 teaspoons raspberry-flavored syrup
(for coffee drinks) or red raspberry syrup
(for pancakes)

¼ cup powdered sugar

Fresh raspberries, if desired

Fresh mint leaves, if desired

*To easily crush granola bars, do not
unwrap; use rolling pin to crush bars.

Pat Freymuth |
Colorado Springs, CO

**Pat Freymuth** adapted her torte recipe from a fat-laden version that was her husband's favorite. The result, she says, is a "rich, dark, creamy chocolate heaven." She serves the torte whenever her husband asks for his favorite dessert or when she has company. "You don't even need to let them know they're eating cholesterol-fighting oats."

# heavenly chocolate-raspberry torte

**12 servings** | Prep Time: **20 minutes** | Start to Finish: **2 hours 25 minutes**

1 Heat oven to 350°F. Lightly spray bottom of 9-inch round cake pan with cooking spray; line bottom with parchment paper. Spray paper and side of pan with cooking spray.

2 Reserve ½ cup of the chocolate chips for glaze; place remaining chips in medium microwavable bowl (or place in top of double boiler). Stir in yogurt until chips are coated. Microwave on High in 1-minute increments, stirring after each, until chips are completely melted (or heat in double boiler over simmering water, stirring frequently, until melted). Stir in crushed granola bars and egg whites until well blended. Pour batter into pan.

3 Bake 20 to 30 minutes or until side of torte has risen and center is shiny but firm when touched (if center rises, torte has been overbaked). Cool in pan on wire rack, about 30 minutes (as torte cools, side will pull away from pan and torte will slightly sink). Refrigerate until chilled, about 1 hour.

4 In small microwavable bowl, microwave reserved ½ cup chocolate chips and the half-and-half on High in 30-second increments, stirring after each, until chips are melted. Cool slightly, about 2 minutes.

5 Place wire rack upside down over pan; turn rack and pan over. Remove pan and parchment paper. Pour chocolate mixture over torte; spread over top and side. Slide torte onto serving plate.

6 In small bowl, mix syrup and sugar. Place in small resealable food-storage plastic bag; seal bag and cut tiny hole in one bottom corner. Drizzle over top of torte in spiral pattern; gently run toothpick back and forth through spiral pattern to feather. Refrigerate until glaze is set and firm to the touch, about 20 minutes.

7 Before serving, garnish tray and/or individual dessert plates with raspberries and mint. Cut torte into wedges with warm, dry knife, cleaning knife between cuts. Store torte in refrigerator.

High Altitude (3,500–6,500 ft): Bake 25 to 30 minutes.

**1 Serving:** Calories 240 (Calories from Fat 90); Total Fat 10g (Saturated Fat 5g; Trans Fat 0g); Cholesterol 0mg; Sodium 90mg; Total Carbohydrate 31g (Dietary Fiber 2g; Sugars 24g); Protein 5g **% Daily Value:** Vitamin A 0%; Vitamin C 0%; Calcium 4%; Iron 6% **Exchanges:** ½ Starch, 1½ Other Carbohydrate, ½ Very Lean Meat, 2 Fat **Carbohydrate Choices:** 2

Southwestern Chicken-Biscuit Pot Pie

**Receta Rica Award: Diane Leigh Kerekes** of Sapulpa, Oklahoma, received this award for creatively using Hispanic-inspired flavors, ingredients or techniques. She also won the Cooking for Two category, taking home $10,000 for her Southwestern Chicken-Biscuit Pot Pie (page 116).

# chapter four

# cooking for two

Table for two, please! These easy-to-fix recipes all make two servings, and you'll find something for every meal of the day. The Grand Prize winner, Anna Ginsberg, was an entry from this category. (See page 128.)

## What's Cooking for Two?

Amateur chefs are refining their appreciation of Hispanic-influenced cuisine, taking steps beyond Mexican dishes into Puerto Rican-, Cuban-, Peruvian- and Spanish-flavored foods. And when contestants entered Mexican-inspired recipes, they called for more authentically Mexican ingredients like squash flowers, salsa verde, achiote paste, poblano peppers and suiza seasoning; and they used techniques like creating sofrito and shredding meats.

Cooking's a passion when you're cooking for two! Home cooks entering this category especially seemed to enjoy cooking, based on the kinds of recipes entered and the preparation details provided.

Whether influenced by big appetites or restaurant-style portions, some entrants were challenged to create recipes sized just for two.

1 can (18.5 oz) ready-to-serve
  southwestern-style chicken soup

¼ teaspoon onion powder

¼ teaspoon garlic powder

¼ teaspoon ground chipotle chiles

Cooking spray

½ cup frozen extra-sweet whole kernel corn
  (from 1-lb bag)

1 package (3 oz) diced cooked chicken
  (⅔ cup)

2 oz Monterey Jack cheese, cut into
  4 (3 × 1 × ⅛-inch) slices

3 tablespoons chopped roasted red bell
  peppers (from jar)

2 frozen southern-style biscuits (from
  25-oz bag)

2 to 4 tablespoons sour cream

1 to 2 tablespoons finely chopped fresh
  chives or green onions

Diane Leigh Kerekes | Sapulpa, OK

**Diane Leigh Kerekes**
says it was her husband's
idea to cook a biscuit in
soup. Diane picked up
the idea and ran . . . all
the way to the Bake-Off® Contest.
When she and her husband first
tasted her new recipe, "we were
astounded," said Diane. She now
serves it monthly by request of son
János. Diane cooks quite a variety of
foods, from those requiring two-day
preparation to hot dogs and French
fries. "But I like the easy and tasty
ones best!"

# southwestern chicken-biscuit pot pie

**2 servings**  |  Prep Time: **20 minutes**  |  Start to Finish: **1 hour 10 minutes**

1  Heat oven to 350°F. Pour soup into 2-cup measuring cup or bowl. Stir in onion powder, garlic powder and ground chipotle chiles.

2  Spray insides of 2 ovenproof 2-cup bowls with cooking spray. Place ¼ cup corn and ⅓ cup chicken in each bowl. Pour about 1 cup soup mixture evenly into bowls. Carefully place 2 cheese slices in center on top of soup in each bowl. Sprinkle 1 tablespoon roasted peppers evenly around cheese in each. Place biscuits over cheese; spray biscuits with cooking spray.

3  Place bowls on cookie sheet; bake 38 to 43 minutes or until biscuits are golden brown and soup bubbles around edges. Cool 5 minutes before serving. Serve topped with sour cream, chives and remaining tablespoon roasted peppers.

High Altitude (3,500–6,500 ft): Bake 43 to 48 minutes.

1 Serving: Calories 570 (Calories from Fat 230); Total Fat 26g (Saturated Fat 11g; Trans Fat 4.5g); Cholesterol 75mg; Sodium 1900mg; Total Carbohydrate 54g (Dietary Fiber 4g; Sugars 7g); Protein 31g  % Daily Value: Vitamin A 30%; Vitamin C 25%; Calcium 25%; Iron 15%  Exchanges: 3 Starch, ½ Other Carbohydrate, 3 Lean Meat, 3 Fat  Carbohydrate Choices: 3½

**Parfaits**

4 pecan crunch crunchy granola bars
   (2 pouches from 8.9-oz box), crushed
   (¾ cup)*

½ cup chopped pecans

1 package (3 oz) cream cheese, softened

½ cup whipped topping

½ cup marshmallow creme (from 7-oz jar)

1 oz white chocolate baking bar, shaved

1 container (6 oz) white chocolate
   strawberry low-fat yogurt

1 cup sliced fresh strawberries

**Garnishes**

Additional strawberry slices

White chocolate curls

Fresh mint leaves

*To easily crush granola bars, do not
unwrap; use rolling pin to crush bars.

Janelle Sperry  |  Bunker Hill, WV

The ovens in the Bake-Off® kitchens seemed much higher the last time **Janelle Sperry** cooked there as a finalist: It was 1982 and she was just 10 years old. After 23 years, she hadn't lost her touch. This time, Janelle entered a simple and versatile parfait, adapted from one of her favorite fruit dips. Yogurt, granola, pecans and white chocolate make it a versatile treat that can be served at any meal or as dessert.

# white chocolate–strawberry yogurt parfaits

**2 servings**  |  Prep Time: **15 minutes**  |  Start to Finish: **15 minutes**

1  In small bowl, mix crushed granola bars and pecans; set aside. In large bowl, beat cream cheese with electric mixer on medium speed until smooth. Beat in whipped topping, marshmallow creme, shaved white chocolate and yogurt until well blended.

2  In each of 2 (14-oz) parfait glasses, layer ¼ cup granola mixture, about ½ cup yogurt mixture and ¼ cup sliced strawberries. Repeat layers. Top each parfait with 1 tablespoon remaining granola mixture. Garnish each with additional strawberry slices, white chocolate curls and mint leaves. Serve immediately.

High Altitude (3,500–6,500 ft): No change.

1 **Serving:** Calories 860 (Calories from Fat 440); Total Fat 49g (Saturated Fat 17g; Trans Fat 0g); Cholesterol 50mg; Sodium 370mg; Total Carbohydrate 89g (Dietary Fiber 7g; Sugars 64g); Protein 15g  **% Daily Value:** Vitamin A 20%; Vitamin C 80%; Calcium 25%; Iron 15%  **Exchanges:** 1 Starch, ½ Fruit, 4 Other Carbohydrate, ½ Skim Milk, 1 High-Fat Meat, 8 Fat  **Carbohydrate Choices:** 6

1 tablespoon butter or vegetable oil

⅓ cup finely chopped onion (1 small)

1 can (10 oz) red enchilada sauce

1 to 3 teaspoons ground cumin

1 can (12.5 oz) chunk chicken breast in water, drained

4 flour tortillas for burritos, 8 inch (from 11.5-oz package)

1 cup shredded pepper Jack cheese (4 oz)

1 cup shredded Cheddar cheese (4 oz)

⅓ cup sliced jalapeño chiles (from jar)

1 can (7 oz) chopped green chiles

Sour cream

# stove-top chicken enchilada lasagna

**2 servings**  |  Prep Time: **15 minutes**  |  Start to Finish: **45 minutes**

1  In 2-quart saucepan, melt butter over medium heat. Add onion; cook 3 to 5 minutes, stirring frequently, until tender. Reserve ¼ cup enchilada sauce; add remaining sauce to onion. Stir in cumin and chicken. Reduce heat to medium-low; simmer uncovered 5 minutes.

2  Lightly grease 10-inch skillet with butter or cooking spray; heat over low heat. Place 1 tortilla in skillet; top evenly with pepper Jack cheese and second tortilla. Spread chicken mixture over second tortilla; top with third tortilla. Sprinkle evenly with Cheddar cheese; top with jalapeño chiles and green chiles. Place fourth tortilla over chiles; spread reserved ¼ cup enchilada sauce over top.

3  Cover skillet; cook over low heat 18 to 20 minutes or until thoroughly heated. Remove from heat; let stand 10 minutes before serving. Cut into 4 wedges; serve topped with sour cream and if desired, several additional jalapeño chile slices.

High Altitude (3,500–6,500 ft): In step 3, cook over medium-low heat 21 to 23 minutes.

1 Serving: Calories 970 (Calories from Fat 510); Total Fat 57g (Saturated Fat 30g; Trans Fat 1.5g); Cholesterol 205mg; Sodium 3040mg; Total Carbohydrate 59g (Dietary Fiber 1g; Sugars 7g); Protein 56g  % Daily Value: Vitamin A 40%; Vitamin C 15%; Calcium 90%; Iron 25%  Exchanges: 3 Starch, 1 Other Carbohydrate, 6½ Medium-Fat Meat, 4½ Fat Carbohydrate Choices: 4

## Laura Ware  |  Fort Worth, TX

A love of enchiladas and quesadillas inspired **Laura Ware** to create this Mexican-style lasagna that doesn't require baking. Cooking hasn't always come easily to Laura. "I had a lot of failures," she said. Her most unusual baking creation was a turkey-flavored Thanksgiving cake with a cranberry cream-cheese frosting. "People were reluctant to try it at first," she recalled. "I thought it would be unique."

4 slices packaged precooked bacon (from 2.1-oz package)

2 frozen extra-large biscuits (from 31.8-oz bag), or 2 frozen southern-style biscuits (from 25-oz bag)

1 can (4.5 oz) chopped green chiles

½ cup shredded sharp Cheddar cheese (2 oz)

2 eggs

Salt and pepper, if desired

1 small tomato, finely chopped (½ cup)

1 tablespoon chopped fresh cilantro

1 tablespoon chopped red onion

1 tablespoon lime juice

Sliced cantaloupe, if desired

# breakfast biscuit cups with green chile salsa

**2 servings**  |  Prep Time: **15 minutes**  |  Start to Finish: **50 minutes**

1 Heat oven to 375°F. Spray 2 (10-oz) custard cups or soufflé dishes with cooking spray. If necessary, heat bacon in microwave on High 15 seconds or until warm and pliable. Line inner side of each custard cup (not bottom) with 2 bacon slices, overlapping as necessary.

2 Gently place frozen biscuit in each cup to fit inside bacon collar. Spoon 1 heaping tablespoon green chiles onto each biscuit; place remaining green chiles in small bowl and set aside. Sprinkle 2 tablespoons cheese over chiles on each biscuit. Carefully crack 1 egg over cheese on each. Sprinkle each with 2 tablespoons remaining cheese to cover; sprinkle with salt and pepper.

3 Place custard cups on cookie sheet; bake 25 to 35 minutes or until biscuits are baked and egg whites are set. Cool in cups 5 minutes. Meanwhile, add tomato, cilantro, onion and lime juice to green chiles in bowl; mix well. Season to taste with salt.

4 Carefully remove bacon-wrapped biscuits from custard cups; place on individual plates. Spoon green chile salsa over top and around sides. Serve with cantaloupe.

High Altitude (3,500–6,500 ft): Heat oven to 400°F. In step 2, do not sprinkle 2 tablespoons remaining cheese over each egg; sprinkle with salt and pepper. In step 3, bake 30 minutes. Sprinkle remaining cheese over eggs; bake about 2 minutes longer or until cheese is melted.

1 Serving: Calories 580 (Calories from Fat 310); Total Fat 35g (Saturated Fat 13g; Trans Fat 6g); Cholesterol 260mg; Sodium 1700mg; Total Carbohydrate 41g (Dietary Fiber 2g; Sugars 6g); Protein 26g  % Daily Value: Vitamin A 25%; Vitamin C 20%; Calcium 25%; Iron 15%  Exchanges: 2 Starch, ½ Other Carbohydrate, 3 Medium-Fat Meat, 4 Fat Carbohydrate Choices: 3

Erin Renouf Mylroie  |  St George, UT

**Erin Renouf Mylroie** counts Southwestern cuisine among her favorites, and this flavorful dish is typical of her cooking style. It's versatile enough for brunch or dinner. Erin's kitchen doubles as a classroom for her home-schooled daughter. And in between parenting, teaching and cooking, she is working on a family cookbook, a labor of love she began in 2000. She sends each section off to relatives as she completes it.

1 package (10 oz) frozen cheesy rice
  & broccoli

1 cup shredded Mexican 4-cheese blend
  (4 oz)

½ cup ranch-flavored sliced almonds

2 tablespoons finely chopped fresh cilantro

1 teaspoon chili powder

½ teaspoon dried Mexican oregano leaves

¼ to ¾ teaspoon salt

3 eggs

4 tablespoons vegetable oil

4 flour tortillas for soft tacos and fajitas,
  6 inch (from 10.5-oz package)

Fresh cilantro sprigs, if desired

Pickled jalapeño-flavored cucumbers, sliced,
  if desired

Chunky-style salsa, if desired

# cheesy rice & broccoli in egg tortillas

**2 servings (2 filled tortillas each)** | Prep Time: **30 minutes** | Start to Finish: **30 minutes**

1 Cook rice and broccoli as directed on box. In medium bowl, mix rice and broccoli, the cheese, almonds, chopped cilantro, ½ teaspoon of the chili powder, ¼ teaspoon of the oregano and ¼ teaspoon of the salt.

2 In pie plate or shallow bowl, beat eggs, remaining chili powder, oregano and remaining salt if desired with fork until well blended.

3 In 10-inch nonstick skillet, heat 1 tablespoon of the oil over medium heat. Dip 1 tortilla into egg mixture, letting egg mixture soak into tortilla; place in hot skillet. Cook until bottom of tortilla is browned, spooning 2 tablespoons egg mixture over tortilla (some egg mixture may run off).

4 Turn tortilla; place about ½ cup rice mixture down center of tortilla. Fold sides of tortilla over rice mixture; press with pancake turner. Turn filled tortilla and press again. Cook 1 to 2 minutes longer or until tortilla is browned and filling is thoroughly heated. Place filled tortilla on plate; cover to keep warm. Repeat making 3 more filled tortillas. Cut each filled tortilla diagonally in half. Garnish with cilantro sprigs; serve with cucumbers and salsa or if desired, serve with green salad.

High Altitude (3,500–6,500 ft): No change.

1 **Serving:** Calories 1070 (Calories from Fat 680); Total Fat 76g (Saturated Fat 20g; Trans Fat 1g); Cholesterol 375mg; Sodium 2320mg; Total Carbohydrate 60g (Dietary Fiber 5g; Sugars 7g); Protein 36g **% Daily Value:** Vitamin A 60%; Vitamin C 10%; Calcium 70%; Iron 35% **Exchanges:** 3½ Starch, ½ Other Carbohydrate, 3½ Medium-Fat Meat, 11 Fat **Carbohydrate Choices:** 4

Loanne Chiu | Fort Worth, TX

**Loanne Chiu**, born into a Chinese family in Indonesia, grew up eating fiery Indonesian fare, mild Chinese foods and some Dutch dishes. Later, at a German university, Loanne yearned for Asian food. There were no Asian groceries and she could not afford to eat at Asian restaurants, so she improvised. Today, this Texan continues to mix and match cuisines. "How about Szechuan chili, Texas spring rolls or Chinese gumbo?" she asked.

1 tablespoon olive oil

1 cup sliced fresh mushrooms

1 small onion, sliced (½ cup)

1 box (10 oz) frozen broccoli in a zesty cheese sauce

⅔ cup ricotta cheese

1 cup chopped cooked chicken

1 can (4 oz) refrigerated crescent dinner rolls (4 rolls)

## Kibby Jackson | Gray, GA

Now that their daughters are living on their own, **Kibby Jackson** and her husband cook what they like. This casserole recipe originated when she combined some of their favorite tastes. "It was good!" said Kibby. Her husband agreed and ate two casseroles. When she began cooking, her "from-scratch" biscuits were "so hard," but her husband gallantly ate them anyway.

# chicken-broccoli au gratin

**2 servings** | Prep Time: **20 minutes** | Start to Finish: **45 minutes**

1 Heat oven to 375°F. In 10-inch skillet, heat oil over medium-high heat. Add mushrooms and onion; cook 5 to 7 minutes, stirring frequently, until tender. Meanwhile, microwave broccoli with cheese sauce as directed on box.

2 Spread ⅓ cup ricotta cheese in bottom of each of 2 ungreased 2-cup au gratin dishes or individual casseroles.* Top each evenly with chicken, mushroom mixture and broccoli with cheese sauce.

3 Unroll dough; separate into 2 rectangles. Place 1 rectangle over top of each dish, tucking corners into dish as needed.

4 Place dishes on cookie sheet; bake 20 to 25 minutes or until tops are golden brown and edges are bubbly.

High Altitude (3,500–6,500 ft): For either au gratin dishes or square glass baking dish: In step 1, cook mushrooms and onion 5 minutes, stirring frequently. Add chicken to mixture; cook and stir 2 minutes longer. In step 4, bake 23 to 28 minutes.

1 **Serving:** Calories 560 (Calories from Fat 240); Total Fat 27g (Saturated Fat 7g; Trans Fat 3g); Cholesterol 70mg; Sodium 1170mg; Total Carbohydrate 43g (Dietary Fiber 3g; Sugars 16g); Protein 38g  % **Daily Value:** Vitamin A 4%; Vitamin C 25%; Calcium 20%; Iron 15% **Exchanges:** 1 Starch, 1 Other Carbohydrate, 2 Vegetable, 4½ Lean Meat, 2 ½ Fat **Carbohydrate Choices:** 3

*Recipe can be made in ungreased 8-inch square (2-quart) glass baking dish. Spread ricotta cheese in dish; top with chicken, mushroom mixture and broccoli with cheese sauce. Arrange dough rectangles over top. Bake as directed.

3 tablespoons maple-flavored syrup

2 tablespoons peach preserves

½ teaspoon Worcestershire sauce

2 bone-in skin-on chicken breasts (1 lb)

¼ teaspoon salt

¼ teaspoon pepper

4 squares frozen homestyle or buttermilk waffles

1 tablespoon butter or margarine

½ cup chopped onion (1 medium)

¼ cup chicken broth

½ teaspoon poultry seasoning

½ teaspoon chopped fresh sage

1 tablespoon beaten egg white

1 box (9 oz) frozen spinach, thawed, drained

1 tablespoon chopped pecans

## Anna Ginsberg | Austin, TX

The idea for her chicken recipe "came like a lightning bolt out of the blue," said Million Dollar Bake-Off® Winner **Anna Ginsberg**. She served it to her husband, who loved it. She prepares this dish when she craves comfort food. Anna is passionate about cooking and baking—especially cookies. She even maintains a blog detailing the cookies she makes. Previously, she worked in advertising, where she unfailingly developed the reputation as "the girl who's always bringing in the cookies."

# baked chicken and spinach stuffing

**2 servings** | Prep Time: **35 minutes** | Start to Finish: **1 hour**

1 Heat oven to 350°F. Spray 9-inch glass pie plate or 8-inch square pan with cooking spray. In small bowl, mix syrup, preserves and Worcestershire sauce. Place chicken, skin side up, in pie plate; sprinkle with salt and pepper. Spoon syrup mixture over chicken.

2 Bake uncovered 40 to 45 minutes. Meanwhile, toast waffles until golden brown. Cool slightly, about 2 minutes. Cut waffles into ¾-inch cubes; set aside. Spray 1-quart casserole with cooking spray (or use 9 × 5-inch nonstick loaf pan; do not spray). In 10-inch nonstick skillet, melt butter over medium heat. Add onion; cook and stir 2 minutes or until tender. Stir in waffle pieces and broth, breaking up waffle pieces slightly to moisten. Sprinkle with poultry seasoning and sage. Remove from heat; cool about 5 minutes. Stir in egg white and spinach. Spoon stuffing into casserole. Sprinkle pecans over top.

3 Twenty minutes before chicken is done, place casserole in oven next to chicken in pie plate. Spoon syrup mixture in pie plate over chicken. Bake chicken and stuffing uncovered 20 to 25 minutes longer or until juice of chicken is clear when thickest part is cut to bone (170°F) and stuffing is thoroughly heated. Spoon remaining syrup mixture in pie plate over chicken. Serve chicken with stuffing.

High Altitude (3,500–6,500 ft): In step 3, after adding stuffing to oven, bake chicken and stuffing 20 to 30 minutes longer.

**1 Serving:** Calories 640 (Calories from Fat 200); Total Fat 22g (Saturated Fat 8g; Trans Fat 1.5g); Cholesterol 105mg; Sodium 1140mg; Total Carbohydrate 68g (Dietary Fiber 5g; Sugars 28g); Protein 42g **% Daily Value:** Vitamin A 210%; Vitamin C 6%; Calcium 15%; Iron 35% **Exchanges:** 2 Starch, 2 Other Carbohydrate, 1 Vegetable, 5 Lean Meat, 1 Fat **Carbohydrate Choices:** 4½

4 slices packaged precooked bacon (from 2.1-oz package)

¼ cup seedless raspberry jam

1 container (6 oz) red raspberry low-fat yogurt

1 tablespoon unsalted butter

4 frozen homestyle waffles (from 12-oz bag)

6 slices (¾ to 1 oz each) Swiss cheese

4 slices (⅓ to ½ oz each) cooked honey ham

4 slices (⅓ to ½ oz each) cooked turkey

Powdered sugar

Courtney Barrett | Lewisville, TX

Even **Courtney Barrett**'s cat likes her cooking. One morning as she prepared breakfast, she saw her tiny kitty scampering off with bacon dangling from its mouth. Courtney's brother is a fan of her cooking, too. He was the first to sample her Bake-Off® sandwich recipe. He enjoyed it so much that he insisted she cook him a second sandwich.

# monte cristos with raspberry yogurt dip

**2 servings (1 sandwich and ½ cup sauce each)** | Prep Time: **20 minutes** | Start to Finish: **20 minutes**

1 Heat bacon as directed on package; set aside. In small bowl, mix jam and yogurt; set aside.

2 In 12-inch skillet, melt butter over medium-low heat. Add 2 waffles; cook 3 to 4 minutes or until ridges are golden brown and tops begin to soften. Turn waffles; add remaining 2 waffles to skillet.

3 On each of first 2 toasted waffles, layer 1 Swiss cheese slice, 2 ham slices, 1 bacon slice, 1 Swiss cheese slice, 1 bacon slice, 2 turkey slices and 1 Swiss cheese slice (evenly arrange cheese so sandwich will hold together). Top each with remaining hot waffle, toasted side down. Cook about 2 minutes or until bottom waffles are browned.

4 Turn sandwiches; cover and cook about 4 minutes longer or until waffles are browned and cheese is melted. Cut sandwiches in half; lightly sprinkle with powdered sugar. Serve with raspberry sauce for dipping.

High Altitude (3,500–6,500 ft): Cook over medium heat.

**1 Serving:** Calories 980 (Calories from Fat 390); Total Fat 43g (Saturated Fat 21g; Trans Fat 4g); Cholesterol 115mg; Sodium 2140mg; Total Carbohydrate 106g (Dietary Fiber 0g; Sugars 43g); Protein 41g **% Daily Value:** Vitamin A 60%; Vitamin C 4%; Calcium 70%; Iron 45% **Exchanges:** 2 Starch, 4½ Other Carbohydrate, ½ Skim Milk, 4½ High-Fat Meat, 1 Fat **Carbohydrate Choices:** 7

2 tablespoons olive oil

2 beef tenderloin steaks, about 1 inch thick
(4 oz each)

½ teaspoon Montreal steak seasoning

4 refrigerated buttermilk biscuits
(2 twin-packs from 21-oz package)

1 egg yolk

1 tablespoon water

1 cup crumbled Gorgonzola cheese (4 oz)

⅛ teaspoon pepper

½ cup whipping cream

½ teaspoon Worcestershire sauce

1 jar (4.5 oz) sliced mushrooms, drained

1½ teaspoons chopped fresh parsley

Kelly Lynne Baxter  |  Olympia, WA

When **Kelly Lynne Baxter** got the Bake-Off® call, she was so "stunned, delighted, honored and flustered" that she had trouble remembering the name of her street. Her recipe idea came from her dad's description of layering meat in a pie crust and her husband's fondness for Gorgonzola butter on steak. "The resulting dish is romantic and elegant," Kelly said. The best cooking advice she ever received was, "When things go wrong, there's always Chinese takeout."

# wrapped tenderloin with gorgonzola-mushroom gravy

**2 servings**  |  Prep Time: **20 minutes**  |  Start to Finish: **35 minutes**

1  Heat oven to 400°F. In 8-inch skillet, heat oil over medium-high heat. Pat steaks dry with paper towel; sprinkle both sides with steak seasoning. Add steaks to skillet; cook 1 to 2 minutes on each side or until browned. Remove steaks from skillet; place on plate.

2  Spray cookie sheet or 13 × 9-inch baking dish with cooking spray. On cookie sheet or in baking dish, roll or press 2 of the biscuits into 5- to 6-inch rounds. Place 1 steak on center of each flattened biscuit. Press remaining 2 biscuits into 5- to 6-inch rounds; place over steaks. Flute or crimp edges with fork to seal. In small bowl, beat egg yolk and water with fork until blended; brush over top biscuits. Bake 14 to 18 minutes or until golden brown.

3  Meanwhile, in 1-quart saucepan, mix cheese, pepper, whipping cream and Worcestershire sauce. Heat to boiling. Reduce heat to medium-low; simmer uncovered, stirring constantly, until cheese is melted. Stir in mushrooms. Keep warm over low heat.

4  Serve half of mushroom gravy over each wrapped steak; sprinkle with parsley.

High Altitude (3,500-6,500 ft): No change.

1 **Serving:** Calories 1130 (Calories from Fat 700); Total Fat 78g (Saturated Fat 34g; Trans Fat 9g); Cholesterol 260mg; Sodium 2300mg; Total Carbohydrate 57g (Dietary Fiber 1g; Sugars 14g); Protein 50g  % **Daily Value:** Vitamin A 25%; Vitamin C 0%; Calcium 35%; Iron 30%  **Exchanges:** 3 Starch, 1 Other Carbohydrate, 6 Medium-Fat Meat, 9 Fat **Carbohydrate Choices:** 4

2 flour tortillas (8 to 10 inch)

5 oz smoked chorizo sausage links,
  coarsely chopped

1 large clove garlic, finely chopped

⅓ cup dry sherry or chicken broth

½ teaspoon chili powder

1 can (19 oz) ready-to-serve black bean soup

1 can (4.5 oz) chopped green chiles

⅓ cup shredded Mexican 4-cheese blend
  (1⅓ oz)

2 tablespoons sour cream

2 tablespoons chopped fresh cilantro

Sita Lepczyk Williams |
Blacksburg, VA

"I'm always trying new things and putting new twists on old recipes," said **Sita Lepczyk Williams**. She started with black bean soup, then added some spicy chorizo sausage, chopped green chiles and seasonings and topped it all with sour cream and chopped cilantro. She served the soup in a tortilla shell baked into a bowl shape. Sita says she received the best cooking advice from her Aunt Wanda, "Go for simplicity."

# black bean–chorizo soup in tortilla bowls

**2 servings (1½ cups soup in 1 tortilla bowl each)** | Prep Time: **25 minutes** | Start to Finish: **25 minutes**

1 Place oven rack in bottom rack position; heat oven to 350°F. Spray 2 (10-oz) ovenproof custard cups with cooking spray; place on cookie sheet.

2 Place tortillas on microwavable plate; cover with microwavable plastic wrap. Microwave on High 45 to 60 seconds, turning after 30 seconds, until very soft. Center tortillas over cups, press into cups so top edges are even. Press tortilla folds against side of each cup to make bowl as large as possible.

3 Bake on bottom oven rack 8 to 10 minutes or until tortillas are stiff enough to hold their shape. Remove tortilla bowls from cups; place on cookie sheet. Return to middle oven rack in oven; bake 5 to 7 minutes longer or until browned and stiff. Remove tortilla bowls from cookie sheet; place on wire rack.

4 Meanwhile, heat 10-inch regular or cast iron skillet over high heat. Add sausage; cook and stir about 30 seconds or until browned. Add garlic; cook and stir 30 to 60 seconds longer. Remove skillet from heat; stir in sherry. Return skillet to high heat; cook and stir 2 to 3 minutes or until liquid has almost evaporated. Stir in chili powder, soup and green chiles. Reduce heat to medium-low; cook, stirring occasionally, until thoroughly heated.

5 Place tortilla bowls on individual plates. Divide soup evenly among bowls. Top each with cheese, sour cream and cilantro. Serve immediately.

High Altitude (3,500–6,500 ft): No change.

1 Serving: Calories 740 (Calories from Fat 360); Total Fat 40g (Saturated Fat 16g; Trans Fat 1g); Cholesterol 85mg; Sodium 2250mg; Total Carbohydrate 62g (Dietary Fiber 10g; Sugars 5g); Protein 34g  % Daily Value: Vitamin A 15%; Vitamin C 10%; Calcium 30%; Iron 35%  Exchanges: 4 Starch, 3 Lean Meat, 6 Fat  Carbohydrate Choices: 4

1 can (19 oz) ready-to-serve tomato basil soup

1 can (7 oz) chopped green chiles

1 cup whipping cream

½ cup refrigerated pasteurized crabmeat (about 3 oz), drained, flaked

1 tablespoon chopped fresh Italian (flat-leaf) parsley

# tomato-crab bisque

**2 servings (2 cups each)** | Prep Time: **15 minutes** | Start to Finish: **15 minutes**

1 In 2-quart saucepan, heat soup and green chiles over medium heat to boiling. Reduce heat to low; beat in whipping cream with wire whisk until blended. Cook just until thoroughly heated (do not boil).

2 Meanwhile, in small microwavable bowl, microwave crabmeat on High 30 to 45 seconds or until thoroughly heated.

3 Ladle soup into individual soup bowls. Top each serving with ¼ cup crabmeat and parsley.

High Altitude (3,500–6,500 ft): No change.

1 Serving: Calories 570 (Calories from Fat 370); Total Fat 41g (Saturated Fat 24g; Trans Fat 1g); Cholesterol 165mg; Sodium 1550mg; Total Carbohydrate 40g (Dietary Fiber 1g; Sugars 21g); Protein 12g  % Daily Value: Vitamin A 50%; Vitamin C 25%; Calcium 20%; Iron 10%  Exchanges: 1 Starch, 1½ Other Carbohydrate, 1 Vegetable, 1 Lean Meat, 7 ½ Fat Carbohydrate Choices: 2½

Robin Spires | Tampa, FL

After enjoying tomato bisque soup at a restaurant, **Robin Spires** decided to try her hand at duplicating it. "I added chiles for a kick and crab for a fresh Florida taste," she said. The result? "It's a delicious and easy dish for two that can be made in a flash." Robin's most memorable cooking experience was a 24-hour nonstop baking marathon during which she created 32 recipes for the Florida State Fair.

1 can (11 oz) refrigerated French loaf

½ teaspoon butter or margarine

1 boneless beef rib eye steak (½ lb), trimmed
of fat, cut into bite-size strips

¼ teaspoon salt

Dash pepper

1 can (18.5 oz) ready-to-serve French
onion soup

1 can (4 oz) mushroom pieces and
stems, drained

½ cup shredded provolone cheese (2 oz)

3 tablespoons chopped green bell pepper

# philly cheese steak onion soup

**2 servings (1¾ cups each)**  |  Prep Time: **10 minutes**  |  Start to Finish: **35 minutes**

1  Heat oven to 350°F. Bake French loaf as directed on can. Meanwhile, in 2-quart saucepan, melt butter over medium heat. Add beef strips; sprinkle with salt and pepper. Cook and stir until browned. Stir in soup; heat to boiling. Reduce heat to medium-low; simmer uncovered 20 minutes.

2  Stir mushrooms into soup; cook until thoroughly heated. Cut 2 (1-inch-thick) diagonal slices from warm loaf; reserve remaining loaf to serve with soup.

3  Set oven control to broil. Ladle soup into 2 (15-oz) ovenproof bowls. Sprinkle 2 tablespoons of the cheese onto each serving. Top each with bread slice. Sprinkle bell pepper and remaining cheese evenly over each.

4  Place bowls on cookie sheet; broil 4 to 6 inches from heat 1 to 2 minutes or until cheese is bubbly and bread is toasted. Serve soup with remaining slices of loaf.

High Altitude (3,500–6,500 ft): No change.

1 Serving: Calories 730 (Calories from Fat 210); Total Fat 23g (Saturated Fat 10g; Trans Fat 2g); Cholesterol 75mg; Sodium 2720mg; Total Carbohydrate 83g (Dietary Fiber 4g; Sugars 13g); Protein 48g  % Daily Value: Vitamin A 8%; Vitamin C 10%; Calcium 25%; Iron 35%  Exchanges: 4½ Starch, 1 Other Carbohydrate, 5 Lean Meat, 1 Fat  Carbohydrate Choices: 5½

Anne Johnson  |  Vincent, OH

**Anne Johnson**'s recipe blends the best flavors of a Philly cheese-steak sandwich with French onion soup. She served it to her young son, who "loved the steak in it," said Anne. Nowadays she prepares it for a quick, late supper. She can cook for two, but she also knows first-hand about large-scale cooking. In college, Anne worked in "the commons," where recipes called for pounds of ingredients, not teaspoons or cups.

2 frozen buttermilk biscuits (from 25-oz package)

1 cup organic frozen sliced peaches (from 10-oz bag), thawed as directed on bag

2 big refrigerated white chunk macadamia nut cookies (from 18-oz package)

2 tablespoons cinnamon-flavored chips

2 tablespoons flaked coconut

1 pint (2 cups) vanilla ice cream, if desired

# aloha peach pies

**2 servings** | Prep Time: **10 minutes** | Start to Finish: **1 Hour 15 Minutes**

1 Place frozen biscuits on small plate and cover with plastic wrap. Allow to stand at room temperature until thawed, about 40 minutes (do not use microwave to thaw).

2 Heat oven to 350°F (325°F for dark cookie sheet). Spray cookie sheet with cooking spray. Place biscuits 3 inches apart on cookie sheet. Press each into 5-inch round with 1/4-inch-high rim around outer edge.

3 For each pie, spoon half of peaches onto biscuit. Crumble 1 cookie dough round evenly over peaches. Top with 1 tablespoon chips and 1 tablespoon coconut. Bake 22 to 28 minutes or until edges are deep golden brown. Cool 5 minutes. Serve warm with ice cream.

High Altitude **(3500-6500 ft): No change.**

1 Serving: Calories 520 (Calories from Fat 230); Total Fat 26g (Saturated Fat 9g, Trans Fat 6g); Cholesterol 10mg; Sodium 720mg; Total Carbohydrate 64g (Dietary Fiber 2g, Sugars 34g); Protein 8g  % Daily Value: Vitamin A 15%; Vitamin C 100%; Calcium 6%; Iron 15%  Exchanges: 2 Starch, 1 Fruit, 1 Other Carbohydrate, 5 Fat  **Carbohydrate Choices:** 4

Candace McMenamin | Lexington, SC

"The smell of a freshly baking peach pie is a wonderful, comforting aroma," said **Candace McMenamin**, but sometimes you don't want a whole pie. She first created her recipe sized for two as a weeknight dessert for her husband. He enjoyed it so much that she decided to teach their two sons to make it for a quick snack. When their oldest son went to college, Candace and her husband often found themselves alone for dinner. She learned to adapt her cooking and downsize recipes to fit their changing lifestyle.

1 can (4 oz) refrigerated crescent dinner rolls (4 rolls)

2 tablespoons finely chopped walnuts

1 tablespoon granulated sugar

1 teaspoon milk

1 container (6 oz) banana crème fat-free yogurt

1 snack-size container (3.5 oz) banana pudding

1 medium banana, sliced

Whipped cream topping (from aerosol can), if desired

Powdered sugar, if desired

# banana crème pastries

**2 servings** | Prep Time: **15 minutes** | Start to Finish: **35 minutes**

1 Heat oven to 375°F. Spray cookie sheet with cooking spray. Unroll dough; separate into 4 triangles. On cookie sheet, make 2 kite shapes by placing longest sides of 2 dough triangles together; press edges to seal.

2 In small bowl, mix walnuts and granulated sugar. Lightly brush dough with milk; sprinkle each evenly with walnut mixture.

3 Bake 8 to 12 minutes or until bottoms are golden brown. Meanwhile, in another small bowl, mix yogurt and pudding until well blended. Stir in banana.

4 Remove pastries from oven. Immediately turn pastries over with pancake turner; gently fold each in half along sealed seam, walnut mixture side out. Remove from cookie sheet; place on wire rack. Cool completely, about 15 minutes.

5 To serve, place pastries on individual dessert plates; fill each with about ¾ cup yogurt mixture. Garnish each with dollop of whipped cream topping; sprinkle with powdered sugar.

High Altitude (3,500–6,500 ft): No change.

1 Serving: Calories 500 (Calories from Fat 180); Total Fat 20g (Saturated Fat 5g; Trans Fat 3.5g); Cholesterol 5mg; Sodium 560mg; Total Carbohydrate 70g (Dietary Fiber 3g; Sugars 40g); Protein 11g  % Daily Value: Vitamin A 8%; Vitamin C 10%; Calcium 20%; Iron 8%  Exchanges: 1 Starch, 1 Fruit, 2 Other Carbohydrate, ½ Skim Milk, ½ High-Fat Meat, 3 Fat  Carbohydrate Choices: 4½

Jaimie Caltabellatta | Midland Park, NJ

During **Jaimie Caltabellatta**'s pregnancy, her family dubbed her baby-in-the-making "Anna Banana." That nickname inspired her to create Banana Crème Pastries, a simple, great-tasting treat. Jaimie credits her mother, a finalist in a previous contest, with encouraging her to enter. "It's do-able," her mother said, "Just try." She did and now says, "I'm a finalist and a believer." And "Anna Banana"? Jaimie and her husband became the proud parents of a baby boy.

2 big refrigerated white chunk macadamia nut cookies (from 18-oz package)

1 cup strawberry ice cream

1 cup organic frozen strawberries (from 10-oz bag), partially thawed

2 tablespoons seedless strawberry jam

2 egg whites (3 to 4 tablespoons)

¼ cup sugar

⅛ teaspoon vanilla

1 tablespoon chocolate-flavor syrup

2 Hershey®'s Kisses® milk chocolates (do not unwrap)

Hershey®'s Kisses,® the conical configuration and the associated trade dresses are registered trademarks used under license.

Carolyn Veazey Shlens |
Seymour, IL

This dessert strikes an appearance that is "spectacular, with elegance and a touch of whimsy," said **Carolyn Veazey Shlens.** She made several changes to the classic baked Alaska recipe, including creating individual servings and using a cookie base and two sauces.

# double-strawberry baked alaska

**2 servings**  |  Prep Time: **15 minutes**  |  Start to Finish: **2 hours 45 minutes**

1 Heat oven to 350°F. Place cookie dough rounds 2 inches apart on ungreased cookie sheet. Bake 14 to 18 minutes or until edges are golden brown. Cool 3 minutes; remove from cookie sheet. Cool completely, about 15 minutes.

2 Place ½ cup ice cream on top of each cookie; place 4 to 5 inches apart on same cookie sheet. Cover loosely; freeze until hardened, at least 1 hour 30 minutes or until serving time. Meanwhile, in small bowl, mix strawberries and jam; refrigerate.

3 To serve, heat oven to 450°F. In small bowl, beat egg whites with electric mixer on high speed until foamy. Gradually beat in sugar until stiff peaks form. Beat in vanilla. Spread egg white mixture over ice cream on each cookie, covering ice cream and cookie edge completely.

4 Bake 4 to 6 minutes or just until meringue is lightly browned. Immediately remove from cookie sheet; place on individual dessert plates. Place strawberries from sauce on side of each dessert; spoon sauce over tops. Drizzle chocolate syrup over each; place wrapped milk chocolate candy on each plate. Serve immediately.

High Altitude (3,500–6,500 ft): No change.

1 Serving: Calories 620 (Calories from Fat 190); Total Fat 21g (Saturated Fat 9g; Trans Fat 2.5g); Cholesterol 45mg; Sodium 240mg; Total Carbohydrate 98g (Dietary Fiber 3g; Sugars 75g); Protein 10g  % Daily Value: Vitamin A 6%; Vitamin C 110%; Calcium 15%; Iron 10%  Exchanges: 1 Starch, 1 Fruit, 3½ Other Carbohydrate, 1 Low-Fat Milk, 3 Fat Carbohydrate Choices: 6½

4 big refrigerated peanut butter cup cookies (from 18-oz package)

¼ cup whipped cream cheese spread (from 8-oz container)

3 tablespoons powdered sugar

2 tablespoons creamy peanut butter

1 container (6 oz) banana thick & creamy low-fat yogurt

½ cup frozen (thawed) whipped topping

1 bar (2.1 oz) chocolate-covered crispy peanut-buttery candy, unwrapped, finely crushed*

¼ cup hot fudge topping

*To easily crush candy bar, unwrap, break into pieces and place in mini food processor; process with on-and-off motions until crushed. Or place unwrapped candy bar in small resealable plastic bag; use rolling pin to crush bar.

Robin Wilson |
Altamonte Springs, FL

Robin Wilson's co-workers are very lucky people. While trying to perfect her Bake-Off® recipe, she'd often bring in as many as six kinds of treats for them to taste. "The staff would try all the goodies and then feel like they needed to go work out!" she said. Her rich parfait recipe "is like eating a peanut-butter cup and a peanut butter–banana sandwich at once."

# fudgy-peanut butter banana parfaits

**2 servings**   |   Prep Time: **15 minutes**   |   Start to Finish: **1 hour 50 minutes**

1 Heat oven to 350°F. Place cookie dough rounds 2 inches apart on ungreased cookie sheet. Bake 14 to 18 minutes or until edges are golden brown. Cool 3 minutes; remove from cookie sheet. Cool completely, about 15 minutes.

2 Meanwhile, in medium bowl, beat cream cheese, powdered sugar, peanut butter and yogurt with electric mixer on low speed until blended. Fold in whipped topping and crushed candy with rubber spatula.

3 In small microwavable bowl, microwave fudge topping on High 25 to 30 seconds or until melted and drizzling consistency. Crumble 1 cookie into each of 2 (12- to 14-oz) parfait glasses.** Top each with about ⅓ cup yogurt mixture; drizzle each with 1 tablespoon fudge topping. Repeat layers. Refrigerate at least 1 hour but no longer than 4 hours before serving.

High Altitude (3,500–6,500 ft): No change.

1 Serving: Calories 1030 (Calories from Fat 450); Total Fat 50g (Saturated Fat 21g; Trans Fat 3.5g); Cholesterol 40mg; Sodium 740mg; Total Carbohydrate 124g (Dietary Fiber 4g; Sugars 92g); Protein 20g  % Daily Value: Vitamin A 15%; Vitamin C 0%; Calcium 20%; Iron 15% Exchanges: 2 Starch, 6 Other Carbohydrate, 2 High-Fat Meat, 6½ Fat Carbohydrate Choices: 8

**Any 12- to 14-ounce tall parfait, dessert or wine glasses can be used.

2 cups Cheerios® cereal

3 tablespoons sugar

2 tablespoons water

2 teaspoons butter, melted

1 cup frozen (thawed) fat-free whipped
     topping (4 oz)

1 tablespoon lime juice

2 containers (6 oz each) Key lime pie
     fat-free yogurt

# key lime parfaits

**2 servings** | Prep Time: **15 minutes** | Start to Finish: **40 minutes**

1 Heat oven to 350°F. Spray cookie sheet and 12 × 12-inch sheet of foil
with cooking spray. In food processor, place cereal and sugar; process
with on-and-off motions until fine crumbs form. Add water and melted
butter; process until thoroughly mixed.

2 Spread cereal mixture evenly in center of cookie sheet. Use foil, sprayed
side down, to press cereal mixture slightly; roll with rolling pin into
12 × 8-inch rectangle, about ⅛ inch thick. With sharp knife, score
mixture into 1-inch squares.

3 Bake 12 to 15 minutes or until squares are golden brown. Cool completely,
about 10 minutes. Meanwhile, in small bowl, place whipped topping; fold
in lime juice until blended.

4 Break cereal mixture apart at scored lines. Reserve 4 cereal squares; crumble
remaining squares into small pieces. In each dessert bowl or 12-oz parfait
glass, layer ¼ cup crumbled cereal squares, half container of yogurt and
scant ¼ cup whipped topping mixture. Repeat layers. Top each parfait with
2 reserved cereal squares.

High Altitude **(3,500–6,500 ft): No change.**

**1 Serving:** Calories 450 (Calories from Fat 60); Total Fat 7g (Saturated Fat 3.5g; Trans Fat 0g); Cholesterol 15mg;
Sodium 360mg; Total Carbohydrate 86g (Dietary Fiber 3g; Sugars 57g); Protein 11g  **% Daily Value:** Vitamin A 25%;
Vitamin C 8%; Calcium 35%; Iron 45%  **Exchanges:** 1 Starch, 4 Other Carbohydrate, 1 Skim Milk, 1 Fat  **Carbohydrate
Choices:** 6

Nancy Heikkila | Russellville, AR

**Nancy Heikkila** and
her family host a cooking
class in their home
several times a month.
International students
from the local university demonstrate
how to prepare dishes from their own
countries. Nancy said she tries to use
ingredients in new ways, and that's
how she originated these parfaits.

**Ronna Farley** of Rockville, Maryland, won $10,000 and a new oven for her yummy Choco-Peanut Butter Cups (page 152).

Choco-Peanut Butter Cups

## chapter five

# simple snacks

Serve up these simple appetizers, snacks and treats at casual gatherings with kids, family or friends.

## What's for Snack Time?

Sweets for the sweet. Recipes for sweet snacks like bars, cookies and snack mixes outnumbered those for savory treats among the entries in the category.

Contestants liked their snacks bursting with flavor, commonly using ingredients like cilantro, fresh ginger and roasted red peppers to boost the taste intensity of their recipes.

Snack time is also crunch time. Cereal and popcorn were a popular combination in snack mixes and as the basis for bars.

Dough it again. Entries turned to refrigerated doughs, like crescent rolls, to make small appetizers or pizzas, often using tried-and-true flavors, like the artichoke and Parmesan cheese combination of a popular dip.

1 roll (16.5 oz) refrigerated peanut
   butter cookies

1 cup white vanilla baking chips (6 oz)

1½ cups creamy peanut butter

1 cup semisweet chocolate chips (6 oz)

4 oats 'n honey crunchy granola bars
   (2 pouches from 8.9-oz box), crushed
   (¾ cup)*

*To easily crush granola bars, do not
unwrap; use rolling pin to crush bars.

Ronna Farley | Rockville, MD

**Ronna Farley** concocted
her recipe by considering
ingredients that would
taste good together.
They're easy to prepare:
"Just press the dough into mini-
muffin cups, bake and top. They're
also unusually delicious," she said.
This is Ronna's second Bake-Off®
Contest: She debuted as a finalist
in 1975! That recipe, Ham and
Cheese Crescent Snacks, earned a
place in the Pillsbury Bake-Off®
Hall of Fame, through consumer
voting conducted for the contest's
50th anniversary.

# choco-peanut butter cups

**24 cookie cups** | Prep Time: **40 minutes** | Start to Finish: **1 hour 40 minutes**

1  Heat oven to 350°F. Grease 24 mini muffin cups with cooking spray or
shortening. Cut cookie dough into 24 slices. Press 1 slice in bottom and
up side of each mini muffin cup, forming ¼-inch rim above top of cup
(dust fingers with flour if necessary). Bake 10 to 15 minutes or until edges
are deep golden brown. Cool in pans on wire racks 5 minutes. With tip of
handle of wooden spoon, press dough down in center of each cup to make
room for 2 tablespoons filling.

2  Meanwhile, in 2-quart saucepan, melt white chips and ¾ cup of the
peanut butter over low heat, stirring constantly. Divide mixture evenly
into cookie cups (about 1 tablespoon each). Refrigerate 10 minutes.

3  In same 2-quart saucepan, melt chocolate chips and remaining ¾ cup
peanut butter over low heat, stirring constantly. Divide chocolate mixture
evenly on top of peanut butter mixture in each cup (about 1 tablespoon
each). Sprinkle crushed granola bars over top of each. Refrigerate until
set, about 1 hour. Remove from muffin cups before serving.

High Altitude (3,500–6,500 ft): Break up cookie dough into bowl; knead or stir ¼ cup
flour into dough. Divide dough into 24 pieces; press 1 piece in each cup.

1 Cookie Cup: Calories 280 (Calories from Fat 150); Total Fat 17g (Saturated Fat 5g; Trans Fat 1g); Cholesterol 0mg;
Sodium 210mg; Total Carbohydrate 27g (Dietary Fiber 2g; Sugars 17g); Protein 7g  % Daily Value: Vitamin A 0%;
Vitamin C 0%; Calcium 2%; Iron 4% Exchanges: 1½ Other Carbohydrate, 1 High-Fat Meat, 2 Fat Carbohydrate Choices: 2

1 tablespoon canola or vegetable oil

2½ lb chicken wings, cut apart at joints, wing tips discarded

2 medium green onions, thinly sliced including tops (about 2 tablespoons)

1 teaspoon crushed red pepper flakes

2 cans (12 oz each) lemon-lime carbonated beverage

1 can (4.5 oz) chopped green chiles, drained

1 package (1.25 oz) taco seasoning mix

10 lettuce leaves, if desired

# cinco de mayo glazed chicken wings

**5 servings (4 chicken wings each)** | Prep Time: **50 minutes** | Start to Finish: **50 minutes**

1 In 12-inch nonstick skillet, heat oil over medium-high heat. Add chicken wings and onions; sprinkle with pepper flakes. Cook uncovered 5 to 8 minutes, stirring occasionally, until browned; drain.

2 Stir in carbonated beverage, green chiles and taco seasoning mix. Increase heat to high; cook uncovered 15 minutes, stirring occasionally. Reduce heat to medium-high; cook 5 to 10 minutes, stirring frequently, until chicken wings are completely glazed, small amount of glaze remains in skillet and juice of chicken is clear when thickest part is cut to bone (180°F).

3 To serve, line serving plate with lettuce; arrange chicken wings over lettuce. Serve immediately.

High Altitude (3,500–6,500 ft): In step 1, cook 8 to 11 minutes.

1 Serving: Calories 350 (Calories from Fat 170); Total Fat 19g (Saturated Fat 5g; Trans Fat 0g); Cholesterol 70mg; Sodium 850mg; Total Carbohydrate 20g (Dietary Fiber 0g; Sugars 14g); Protein 23g **% Daily Value:** Vitamin A 8%; Vitamin C 6%; Calcium 4%; Iron 10% **Exchanges:** 1½ Other Carbohydrate, 3½ Medium-Fat Meat **Carbohydrate Choices:** 1

Linda Drumm | Victor, ID

English-born **Linda Drumm** and her father made pork pies when she was a girl. Now she lives in a log home in the mountains of Idaho. According to Linda, it's not unusual to see moose, bear, elk and other "critters." She first served this chicken wing recipe to her husband on Cinco de Mayo and got "a big thumbs up." "Everybody loves this recipe," she said, "including my grandchildren."

1 box (9 oz) frozen spinach

1 egg, beaten

1 cup shredded Parmesan cheese (4 oz)

1 cup shredded mozzarella cheese (4 oz)

1 teaspoon salt

1 teaspoon onion powder

1 teaspoon garlic powder

1 teaspoon dried oregano leaves

½ cup sour cream

2 tablespoons extra-virgin olive oil

1 container (15 oz) ricotta cheese

2 cups all-purpose flour

Vegetable oil for deep frying

¾ cup Italian style dry bread crumbs

1 jar (25.5 oz) organic garden vegetable
   pasta sauce, heated

Ann Waller I Conroe, TX

The idea for her Bake-Off® recipe came to **Ann Waller** after watching a TV chef roll a risotto mixture in bread crumbs and fry it. She liked the idea of a crunchy coating on the outside with melted cheese on the inside, so she began experimenting. Sure enough, "something good happened," she said. The result was addicting: "I end up eating six to ten of these."

# spinach-cheese balls with pasta sauce

**20 servings (2 balls and 3 tablespoons sauce each)** | Prep Time: **1 hour** | Start to Finish: **1 hour**

1 Remove frozen spinach from pouch; place in colander. Rinse with warm water until thawed; drain well. Squeeze spinach dry with paper towel.

2 Meanwhile, in large bowl, mix egg, both cheeses, salt, onion powder, garlic powder, oregano, sour cream, oil and ricotta cheese until well blended. Add spinach to cheese mixture; mix well. Stir in flour, 1 cup at a time, until well blended.

3 Fill 10-inch skillet half full with oil; heat over medium heat until candy/deep-fry thermometer reads 350°F. (Or use deep fryer; add oil to fill line and heat to 350°F.)

4 Meanwhile, place bread crumbs in small bowl. Shape spinach-cheese mixture into 1½-inch balls (about 40), using about 1½ tablespoons for each; roll in bread crumbs and place on cookie sheet.

5 Fry 6 balls at a time 4 to 6 minutes, turning as necessary, until golden brown. With slotted spoon, remove balls from skillet; place on paper towels to drain. Cool 2 minutes before serving; serve with warm pasta sauce for dipping.

High Altitude (3,500-6,500 ft): No change.

1 Serving: Calories 220 (Calories from Fat 110); Total Fat 12g (Saturated Fat 4.5g; Trans Fat 0g); Cholesterol 30mg; Sodium 450mg; Total Carbohydrate 18g (Dietary Fiber 1g; Sugars 2g); Protein 9g  % Daily Value: Vitamin A 30%; Vitamin C 2%; Calcium 20%; Iron 8% Exchanges: 1 Starch, 1 Medium-Fat Meat, 1½ Fat Carbohydrate Choices: 1

½ cup whipped cream cheese spread (from 8-oz container)

1 tablespoon fresh lemon juice

1 to 2 teaspoons red pepper sauce

¼ cup finely shredded mild Cheddar cheese (1 oz)

2 tablespoons finely chopped green onions (2 medium)

1 teaspoon paprika

½ cup garlic-herb dry bread crumbs

3 cans (6 oz each) white crabmeat, well drained

1 can (11 oz) refrigerated original breadsticks

1 egg, slightly beaten

# deviled crab and cheese rolls

6 sandwiches  |  Prep Time: **10 minutes**  |  Start to Finish: **50 minutes**

1  Heat oven to 350°F. Spray cookie sheet with cooking spray or line with a silicone baking mat. In medium bowl, mix cream cheese, lemon juice and red pepper sauce until smooth. Stir in Cheddar cheese, onions and paprika. Reserve 2 tablespoons bread crumbs for topping; stir remaining bread crumbs into cream cheese mixture. Gently stir in crabmeat. Shape crabmeat mixture into 6 balls, using about ⅓ cup mixture for each; flatten slightly.

2  Unroll dough; separate into 6 (2-breadstick) portions. Seal seam halfway up length of each portion; place 1 ball on sealed side of each. Holding dough and ball in one hand, stretch dough strips over balls, crisscrossing and tucking ends under opposite side; place on cookie sheet.

3  Lightly brush tops and sides of dough with beaten egg; sprinkle with reserved 2 tablespoons bread crumbs.

4  Bake 20 to 30 minutes or until golden brown. Cool 10 minutes. Serve warm.

High Altitude (3,500–6,500 ft): No change.

1 Sandwich: Calories 330 (Calories from Fat 100); Total Fat 11g (Saturated Fat 5g; Trans Fat 0.5g); Cholesterol 120mg; Sodium 890mg; Total Carbohydrate 33g (Dietary Fiber 0g; Sugars 4g); Protein 24g  **% Daily Value:** Vitamin A 10%; Vitamin C 2%; Calcium 15%; Iron 15%  **Exchanges:** 2 Starch, 2½ Lean Meat, ½ Fat  **Carbohydrate Choices:** 2

Michael W. Weaver  |
San Francisco, CA

**Michael W. Weaver** enjoyed his first taste of spicy crab rolls when visiting the Cuban sector of Tampa, Florida. For this recipe, he wanted to keep the rolls' intense flavor but lose some of the preparation steps. By using refrigerated dough, he succeeded and won a trip to the Bake-Off® Contest after entering for 30 years. Michael specializes in pies and follows his mother's advice: "Don't overwork your pastry dough!"

2 cups shredded Colby-Monterey Jack
cheese blend (8 oz)

1 cup sour cream

1 tablespoon lime juice

¼ teaspoon chili powder

12 jalapeño slices (from a jar), finely chopped

1 can (18.5 oz) chicken cheese enchilada
flavor soup with reduced carbohydrates
or southwestern-style chicken soup

1 can (14.5 oz) organic diced tomatoes with
basil and garlic, well drained

1 can (4.5 oz) chopped green chiles

1 package (8 oz) cream cheese, softened

1 package (1.25 oz) taco seasoning mix

1 bag (13½ oz) tortilla chips

# fiesta dip

**24 servings (¼ cup dip and 14 chips each)** | Prep Time: **15 minutes** | Start to
Finish: **55 minutes**

1 Heat oven to 350°F. In large bowl, beat all ingredients except chips with
electric mixer on low speed until well blended. Pour into 13 × 9-inch
(3-quart) glass baking dish.

2 Bake 30 to 40 minutes or just until bubbly around edges. Let stand
10 minutes; stir before serving, if desired. Serve with tortilla chips. Store
in refrigerator.

High Altitude (3,500–6,500 ft): Bake 35 to 45 minutes.

**1 Serving:** Calories 200 (Calories from Fat 120); Total Fat 14g (Saturated Fat 6g; Trans Fat 0g); Cholesterol 30mg;
Sodium 470mg; Total Carbohydrate 14g (Dietary Fiber 0g; Sugars 2g); Protein 5g  **% Daily Value:** Vitamin A 10%;
Vitamin C 4%; Calcium 10%; Iron 6%  **Exchanges:** 1 Starch, 2½ Fat  **Carbohydrate Choices:** 1

Winona Garrison |
Douglasville, GA

Yes, **Winona Garrison**'s
husband agreed, she could
get a new mixer if she
reached the Bake-Off®
finals. Winona created her
dip, then served it to her husband. He
didn't think it was spicy enough, so
she "kicked up" the heat with jalapeño
slices. "Looks like I get a new, top-of-
the-line mixer!" she said.

6 tablespoons butter or margarine

1 teaspoon garlic powder

2 tablespoons soy sauce

1 package (1 oz) chow mein oriental
seasoning mix

4 cups Corn Chex® cereal

4 cups crispy horn-shaped corn snacks

2 cups chow mein noodles

1 cup pretzel sticks

1 cup salted peanuts

1 cup wasabi peas

# oriental snack mix

**28 servings (½ cup each)**  |  Prep Time: **10 minutes**  |  Start to Finish: **1 hour 20 minutes**

1 Heat oven to 250°F. In 1-quart saucepan, melt butter over medium
heat. Remove from heat. Stir in garlic powder, soy sauce and chow mein
seasoning mix with wire whisk until well mixed.

2 In large roasting pan, mix remaining ingredients except wasabi peas. Pour
butter mixture over cereal mixture; toss evenly to coat.

3 Bake 50 to 55 minutes, stirring every 15 minutes, until mixture looks
dry and crisp. Pour mixture onto paper towels. Cool 15 minutes. Stir in
wasabi peas before serving. Store in tightly covered container.

High Altitude (3,500–6,500 ft): No change.

1 **Serving:** Calories 130 (Calories from Fat 70); Total Fat 8g (Saturated Fat 3g; Trans Fat 0g); Cholesterol 5mg;
Sodium 310mg; Total Carbohydrate 12g (Dietary Fiber 1g; Sugars 3g); Protein 3g  % **Daily Value:** Vitamin A 4%;
Vitamin C 0%; Calcium 0%; Iron 10%  **Exchanges:** 1 Starch, 1½ Fat  **Carbohydrate Choices:** 1

Michelle Grosella  |  Perkasie, PA

"I don't usually make salty
snacks," said **Michelle
Grosella**, who's more
apt to whip up cookies,
brownies and other
sweet treats. Nevertheless, she took
the snack mix idea, changed the
seasoning and added different
ingredients. Voilà! Oriental Snack
Mix. "I had my husband try it," she
said. "The more he ate, the more he
liked it." Her recipe is so quick and
easy that anyone can make it.

2 cups Cheerios® cereal

2 cups Cinnamon Toast Crunch® cereal

2 cups oats

1 cup sliced almonds

½ cup butter or margarine

¼ cup packed brown sugar

⅓ cup real maple or maple-flavored syrup

# cereal-almond brittle

**14 servings (½ cup each)**  |  Prep Time: **15 minutes**  |  Start to Finish: **1 hour 10 minutes**

1 Heat oven to 300°F. Line 1 large (17 × 14-inch) cookie sheet or 2 (15 × 10 × 1-inch) pans with foil; spray foil with cooking spray. In large bowl, mix both cereals, the oats and almonds; set aside.

2 In 1-quart saucepan, heat butter, brown sugar and syrup over medium heat, stirring frequently, until butter is melted and mixture boils. Pour over cereal mixture; stir until well coated. Spread mixture evenly on cookie sheet with rubber spatula until about ½ inch thick.

3 Bake 35 to 40 minutes or until almonds are golden brown. Cool completely, about 15 minutes. Break into pieces with fingers. Store in tightly covered container.

High Altitude (3,500–6,500 ft): No change.

1 Serving: Calories 220 (Calories from Fat 100); Total Fat 12g (Saturated Fat 4.5g; Trans Fat 0g); Cholesterol 15mg; Sodium 120mg; Total Carbohydrate 26g (Dietary Fiber 3g; Sugars 11g); Protein 4g  % Daily Value: Vitamin A 8%; Vitamin C 0%; Calcium 6%; Iron 15%  Exchanges: ½ Starch, 1 Other Carbohydrate, ½ High-Fat Meat, 1½ Fat  Carbohydrate Choices: 2

Enny Williams  |  Honolulu, HI

"Every Christmas, I make this to give away to my friends as a gift," said **Enny Williams**. It's sweet and simple, with a satisfying crunch. The quick preparation stands in contrast to Enny's native Indonesian cuisine. She notes that with its thousands of inhabited islands, the Republic of Indonesia represents a vast range of foods and culinary traditions. Since traditional Indonesian foods have so many different spices, Enny explained, inexperienced cooks need plenty of patience.

1 package (18 oz) big refrigerated white chunk macadamia nut cookies

1 can (14 oz) sweetened condensed milk (not evaporated)

1 container (6 oz) piña colada low-fat yogurt

1 bag (6 to 7 oz) mixed tropical dried fruits

1 jar (6 oz) dry-roasted macadamia nuts, coarsely chopped

¾ cup white vanilla baking chips (4½ oz)

1 cup flaked coconut

# tropical fruit bars

**36 bars**  |  Prep Time: **15 minutes**  |  Start to Finish: **2 hours 25 minutes**

1  Heat oven to 350°F (325°F for dark pan). Grease 13 × 9-inch pan with shortening or cooking spray. Place cookie dough rounds in pan. With floured fingers, press dough in pan to form crust.

2  In medium bowl, mix condensed milk and yogurt until well blended. Spread over crust to edges of pan. Sprinkle with remaining ingredients in order listed.

3  Bake 30 to 40 minutes or until edges are golden brown. Cool completely, about 1 hour 30 minutes. Cut into 6 rows by 6 rows. Store in refrigerator.

High Altitude (3,500-6,500 ft): Bake 35 to 45 minutes.

1 Bar: Calories 190 (Calories from Fat 90); Total Fat 10g (Saturated Fat 4g; Trans Fat 0.5g); Cholesterol 5mg; Sodium 80mg; Total Carbohydrate 23g (Dietary Fiber 0g; Sugars 18g); Protein 3g **% Daily Value:** Vitamin A 2%; Vitamin C 0%; Calcium 6%; Iron 2% **Exchanges:** 1 Starch, ½ Other Carbohydrate, 2 Fat **Carbohydrate Choices:** 1½

Ann Hobert  |  Westwood Hills, KS

**Ann Hobert** decided to make a tropical cookie and opted to incorporate one of her favorite cookie flavors, white chocolate macadamia nut. She first served these fruit bars at a get-together for family, who thought they were "wonderful."

1 roll (16.5 oz) refrigerated sugar cookies

1 cup lemon curd (from 11¼- to 12-oz jar)

1 package (3 oz) cream cheese (⅓ cup), softened

½ cup marshmallow creme

1 container (6 oz) French vanilla low-fat yogurt

1 cup frozen (thawed) whipped topping

# mock lemon meringue bars

**24 bars** | Prep Time: **15 minutes** | Start to Finish: **2 hours 5 minutes**

1 Heat oven to 350°F. Grease 13 × 9-inch pan with shortening or cooking spray. Break up cookie dough into pan; press in bottom to form crust. Bake 15 to 20 minutes or until edges are golden brown and center is set. Cool on wire rack 30 minutes.

2 Spread lemon curd over cooled baked crust. In large bowl, beat with wooden spoon, cream cheese, marshmallow creme and yogurt until well blended. Fold in whipped topping. Spread over lemon curd, swirling to resemble meringue topping. Refrigerate at least 1 hour or until serving time. Cut into 6 rows by 4 rows. Store in refrigerator.

High Altitude (3,500–6,500 ft): Before pressing cookie dough in pan, knead or stir 3 tablespoons flour into dough.

1 **Bar:** Calories 170 (Calories from Fat 60); Total Fat 7g (Saturated Fat 2.5g; Trans Fat 1g); Cholesterol 20mg; Sodium 85mg; Total Carbohydrate 26g (Dietary Fiber 0g; Sugars 18g); Protein 1g  % **Daily Value:** Vitamin A 0%; Vitamin C 0%; Calcium 0%; Iron 2% **Exchanges:** ½ Starch, 1 Other Carbohydrate, 1½ Fat **Carbohydrate Choices:** 2

Robin Janine Peterson | Peoria, AZ

**Robin Janine Peterson** once sang in the Super Bowl half-time show. Now, the folks who sample these bars are singing praises for the tart-sweet treat. While many other children tuned in to cartoons on Saturday mornings, young Robin watched cooking shows. "Even as a girl, I would always be in the kitchen, talking out loud, pretending I had my own show."

Laura Stensberg of Marshfield, Wisconsin, brought a recipe for delectable Peanut Butter Truffle Tart (page 188) to the contest and took home $10,000 and a new oven for her kitchen!

Peanut Butter Truffle Tart

*chapter six*

# weekends made special

Make your weekends special with these simple-to-prepare recipes you can enjoy with family and friends.

## What Makes the Weekend Special?

Contestants made their weekends special by taking more time with recipes, experimenting with "special-occasion" ingredients and preparing rich, full-flavored dishes.

Perhaps in tribute to the Sunshine State, home of this year's Bake-Off® Contest finals, recipes often used citrus fruits like orange, lemon and lime to make both sweet and savory dishes.

Contestants created new recipe ideas by melding time-honored comfort foods with fusion flavors. Think Asian-influenced tuna noodle casserole, Mediterranean pizza and Mexican-style spaghetti and meatballs.

Regional American cuisine, including gumbos, corn puddings and wild game dishes, also made a strong appearance among the entries.

1 roll (16.5 oz) refrigerated peanut
   butter cookies

6 peanut butter crunchy granola bars
   (3 pouches from 8.9-oz box), crushed
   (1 heaping cup)*

2 bags (12 oz each) semisweet chocolate
   chips (4 cups)

1 cup whipping cream

½ cup crunchy peanut butter

⅓ cup chopped peanuts or 1 package (2 oz)
   nut topping

*To easily crush granola bars, do not
unwrap; use rolling pin to crush bars.

Laura Stensberg | Marshfield, WI

"Sudden cravings can be
the source of inspiration
for a cook," **Laura
Stensberg** said. "I was
craving peanut butter
cups and thought about how to make
the ultimate creation using peanut
butter and chocolate." Although she
normally cooks low-fat, her taste for
something rich and indulgent led her
to create this decadent tart.

# peanut butter truffle tart

**16 servings** | Prep Time: **25 minutes** | Start to Finish: **3 hours 25 minutes**

1 Heat oven to 350°F. In large bowl, break up cookie dough. Stir or knead in crushed granola bars until well mixed. Press dough in bottom and up side of ungreased 10-inch tart pan with removable bottom or 13 × 9-inch pan. Bake 12 to 17 minutes or until light golden brown.

2 With back of spoon, press down crust on bottom and side; bake 3 to 5 minutes longer or until deep golden brown. Press down crust again with spoon. Cool 3 minutes.

3 Meanwhile, in large microwavable bowl, microwave chocolate chips and whipping cream on High 1 minute. Stir; microwave 1 to 2 minutes longer, stirring every 30 seconds to prevent chocolate from burning, until completely melted and smooth. In small microwavable bowl, microwave peanut butter on High 1 minute or until melted; stir.

4 Spread warm peanut butter in bottom of crust. Pour chocolate mixture over peanut butter mixture. Sprinkle peanuts evenly over top. Refrigerate at least 2 hours or until serving time. For easier cutting, let tart stand at room temperature 15 minutes before serving. Store in refrigerator.

High Altitude (3,500–6,500 ft): No change.

1 Serving: Calories 520 (Calories from Fat 270); Total Fat 30g (Saturated Fat 13g; Trans Fat 1.5g); Cholesterol 20mg; Sodium 240mg; Total Carbohydrate 54g (Dietary Fiber 4g; Sugars 36g); Protein 8g  % Daily Value: Vitamin A 4%; Vitamin C 0%; Calcium 4%; Iron 10%  Exchanges: 1 Starch, 2½ Other Carbohydrate, ½ High-Fat Meat, 5 Fat  Carbohydrate Choices: 3½

**Tortilla Strips**

Vegetable oil for frying

4 corn tortillas

**Salad**

16 leaves red or green leaf lettuce (about 1 head)

1 large yellow or orange bell pepper, cut into thin bite-size strips

1 large mango, peeled, seeded and cut into chunks

1 large avocado, pitted, peeled and cut into thin slices

2 large plum (Roma) tomatoes, finely chopped

1 can (15 oz) black beans

1 cup shredded pepper Jack cheese (4 oz)

**Chicken**

4 boneless skinless chicken breasts, cut into ¼-inch-wide strips

1 package (1.25 oz) 40%-less-sodium taco seasoning mix

1 teaspoon ground chipotle chili powder

2 tablespoons water

**Dressing**

⅓ cup vegetable oil

⅓ cup lime juice

2 tablespoons honey

⅓ cup loosely packed cilantro leaves and stems

2 teaspoons Dijon mustard

Dash salt

Heidi Vawdrey | Riverton, UT

**Heidi Vawdrey** is fascinated by other people and cultures. She traces her English lineage back to Ethelred the Unready, but as a nurse who works with the local emergency response team, she's prepared for anything. Heidi also is well prepared in the kitchen, where she learned to cook by helping her mother prepare meals for the family's 12 children.

# chicken fiesta salad

**4 servings (4 lettuce leaves, 3 cups salad)**  |  Prep Time: **1 hour**  |  Start to Finish: **1 hour**

1  In 8-inch skillet, heat ½ inch oil for frying over medium heat. With pizza cutter, cut corn tortillas into ¼-inch-wide strips. Fry strips in batches in hot oil 1 to 2 minutes or until golden and crisp. With tongs, place fried tortilla strips on paper towels to drain.

2  On individual plates, evenly layer lettuce, bell pepper, mango, avocado, tomatoes, beans and cheese.

3  Lightly spray 10-inch skillet with cooking spray. Add chicken strips; sprinkle with taco seasoning mix, chipotle chili powder and water. Cook uncovered over medium heat 5 to 6 minutes, stirring occasionally, until chicken is no longer pink in center. Set aside.

4  In food processor or blender, process all dressing ingredients until well blended and cilantro is finely chopped. Arrange chicken evenly over salads. Drizzle about 3 tablespoons dressing over each salad. Top each evenly with tortilla strips.

High Altitude (3,500–6,500 ft): In steps 1 and 3, cook over medium-high heat.

1 **Serving:** Calories 880 (Calories from Fat 420); Total Fat 47g (Saturated Fat 11g; Trans Fat 0g); Cholesterol 100mg; Sodium 1330mg; Total Carbohydrate 71g (Dietary Fiber 13g; Sugars 23g); Protein 45g **% Daily Value:** Vitamin A 130%; Vitamin C 200%; Calcium 35%; Iron 35% **Exchanges:** 3 Starch, 1½ Other Carbohydrate, 1 Vegetable, 5 Very Lean Meat, 8 Fat **Carbohydrate Choices:** 5

1 bag (10 oz) organic frozen raspberries

½ cup oil and vinegar dressing

¼ cup chopped pecans

1 tablespoon packed brown sugar

2 tablespoons mayonnaise or salad dressing

2 tablespoons maple-flavored syrup or real maple syrup

4 cinnamon crunchy granola bars (2 pouches from 8.9-oz box), finely crushed (¾ cup)*

1 egg

1 lb uncooked chicken breast tenders (not breaded)

½ teaspoon salt

⅛ teaspoon pepper

3 tablespoon vegetable oil

1 bag (10 oz) or 2 bags (5 oz each) mixed baby salad greens

½ cup thinly sliced red onion

2 slices (¾ to 1 oz each) Swiss cheese, cut into thin julienne strips

¼ cup pecan halves, toasted** or glazed

*To crush granola bars, unwrap and place in small resealable food-storage plastic bag; use rolling pin to finely crush bars.

**To toast pecans, bake uncovered in ungreased shallow pan in 350°F oven about 10 minutes, stirring occasionally, until golden brown.

Holly Young | Bountiful, UT

"This is not your typical dinner salad," said **Holly Young**. Its unique mixture of flavors and textures "makes you feel like you're eating a restaurant 'special-of-the-house' in the comfort of your own home." Her specialties are salads, cookies, sandwiches—and once, a very unusual cake. For her daughter's "Under the Sea" party she made a giant, octopus-shaped cake that served 30 people.

# nutty chicken dinner salad

**4 servings** | Prep Time: **40 minutes** | Start to Finish: **40 minutes**

1 Spread frozen raspberries on paper towel; let stand to thaw while making dressing and salad. In small bowl, mix dressing, chopped pecans, brown sugar, mayonnaise and syrup with wire whisk until well blended. Refrigerate until serving time.

2 Place finely crushed granola bars on paper plate or in pie plate. In shallow bowl or another pie plate, beat egg with fork. Sprinkle chicken with salt and pepper.

3 In 12-inch nonstick skillet, heat oil over medium heat. Add chicken to beaten egg; stir to coat. Dip each chicken strip lightly into crushed granola bars; add to skillet. Cook 6 to 8 minutes, turning once, until chicken is no longer pink in center and browned on all sides. Remove from skillet; drain on paper towels.

4 In large serving bowl, mix salad greens, onion, cheese and thawed raspberries. Toss, adding only enough dressing to evenly coat ingredients. Arrange greens mixture on individual plates. Place chicken evenly over greens. Arrange pecan halves on top. Drizzle with remaining dressing.

High Altitude (3,500–6,500 ft): In step 3, cook over medium-high heat.

1 Serving: Calories 750 (Calories from Fat 440); Total Fat 49g (Saturated Fat 8g; Trans Fat 0g); Cholesterol 140mg; Sodium 810mg; Total Carbohydrate 44g (Dietary Fiber 9g; Sugars 22g); Protein 35g  % Daily Value: Vitamin A 80%; Vitamin C 50%; Calcium 20%; Iron 20%  Exchanges: 1½ Starch, 1 Other Carbohydrate, 1 Vegetable, 4 Very Lean Meat, 9 Fat  Carbohydrate Choices: 3

3 tablespoons olive oil

6 boneless skinless chicken breasts (1½ lb), cut into bite-size pieces

1 medium onion, chopped (½ cup)

5 medium cloves garlic, finely chopped (2½ teaspoons)

12 corn tortillas (6 inch), torn or cut into small pieces (2½ cups)

1 cup sour cream

1 can (19 oz) ready-to-serve hearty tomato soup

1 can (15.25 oz) whole kernel corn, drained

1 can (15 oz) black beans, drained, rinsed

1 can (4.5 oz) chopped green chiles

1 package (1.25 oz) taco seasoning mix

½ to 1 teaspoon salt

1 teaspoon ground cumin

¼ teaspoon pepper

2 cups shredded Colby-Monterey Jack cheese blend (8 oz)

1 can (2¼ oz) sliced ripe olives, drained

1 to 2 heads romaine lettuce, shredded (about 16 cups)

4 tomatoes, chopped (3 cups)

8 medium green onions, chopped (½ cup)

Mango-peach salsa, if desired

Susan Bazan I Sequim, WA

**Susan Bazan** used her family's preference for Mexican food as a guide in creating this recipe. Like other recipes that Susan favors, her taco salad tastes "gourmet" but is simple to prepare. She once ventured on her own to Europe for a two-week trip that included renting and driving a car. "After the trip, I knew I could take care of myself."

# baked taco salad

**10 servings (2 cups salad and 1 cup taco mixture each)** I Prep Time: **45 minutes** I Start to Finish: **1 hour 15 minutes**

1 Heat oven to 350°F. Spray 13 × 9-inch (3-quart) glass baking dish with cooking spray. In 12-inch skillet, heat oil over medium-high heat. Add chicken, onion and garlic; cook about 8 minutes, stirring frequently, until chicken is no longer pink in center. Remove skillet from heat.

2 Stir in tortillas, sour cream, soup, corn, beans, green chiles, taco seasoning mix, salt, cumin and pepper. Pour into baking dish. Sprinkle with cheese and olives.

3 Cover tightly with foil; bake 30 minutes. Uncover; bake 15 minutes longer or until cheese is melted and mixture is bubbly.

4 In 6-quart bowl, mix lettuce, tomatoes and green onions. Divide lettuce mixture evenly among individual plates. Top each with baked taco mixture and mango-peach salsa.

High Altitude (3,500–6,500 ft): In step 2, do not add cheese and olives. In step 3, after uncovering baking dish, sprinkle with cheese and olives; bake 15 minutes longer.

1 Serving: Calories 490 (Calories from Fat 180); Total Fat 20g (Saturated Fat 9g; Trans Fat 0g); Cholesterol 80mg; Sodium 1230mg; Total Carbohydrate 48g (Dietary Fiber 9g; Sugars 10g); Protein 30g **% Daily Value:** Vitamin A 130%; Vitamin C 70%; Calcium 35%; Iron 25% **Exchanges:** 2½ Starch, 2 Vegetable, 2½ Very Lean Meat, 3½ Fat **Carbohydrate Choices:** 3

1½ cups water

1 box (6.4 oz) chicken fried rice skillet-meal mix for chicken

½ cup frozen sweet peas (from 1-lb bag)

1 bag (12 oz) frozen cooked cocktail shrimp (60 to 80 count/lb), thawed

¾ cup chopped fresh cilantro

¾ cup sliced pimiento-stuffed green olives

½ cup chopped red onion

2 medium tomatoes, chopped (1½ cups)

1 large Anaheim chile, finely chopped (3 tablespoons)

5 tablespoons balsamic vinegar

2 tablespoons vegetable oil

1 can (15 oz) black beans, drained, rinsed

1 can (11 oz) vacuum-packed white shoepeg corn, drained

# shrimp and rice salad

**6 servings (1⅔ cups each)** | Prep Time: **25 minutes** | Start to Finish: **3 hours 45 minutes**

1 In 10-inch skillet, heat water, uncooked rice and seasoning mix to boiling over high heat, stirring occasionally. Reduce heat to low; cover and simmer 7 minutes.

2 Stir in frozen peas. Cover; cook 3 to 5 minutes longer or until water is completely absorbed. Pour rice mixture into large bowl. Cool about 15 minutes.

3 Stir in all remaining ingredients. Cover; refrigerate 3 to 4 hours before serving.

High Altitude (3,500–6,500 ft): Make rice following High Altitude directions on skillet-meal box.

1 Serving: Calories 400 (Calories from Fat 80); Total Fat 9g (Saturated Fat 1.5g; Trans Fat 0g); Cholesterol 110mg; Sodium 1190mg; Total Carbohydrate 57g (Dietary Fiber 7g; Sugars 7g); Protein 23g  % Daily Value: Vitamin A 25%; Vitamin C 20%; Calcium 15%; Iron 30%  Exchanges: 3 Starch, ½ Other Carbohydrate, 2 Very Lean Meat, 1½ Fat Carbohydrate Choices: 4

---

Nina Hutchison | Windsor, CA

Born in Germany and of Russian (mostly) and Greek heritage, **Nina Hutchison** recalled helping her mother turn out large quantities of piroshkies for holidays. In junior high, she also cooked dinners after school. She once hiked to the famous Burgess Shale fossil site in Canada, went on an archaeological dig and plastered a dinosaur bone.

6 cups uncooked rotini pasta (1 lb)

1 to 2 tablespoons grated lime peel (from 2 medium limes)

3 to 4 tablespoons lime juice (from 2 medium limes)

1 cup ranch dressing

1 package (1.25 oz) taco seasoning mix

1 large avocado, pitted, peeled and finely chopped

1 pint (2 cups) cherry or grape tomatoes, cut in half

1 cup shredded Cheddar cheese (4 oz)

2 tablespoons finely chopped fresh cilantro

2 medium green onions, sliced (including tops)

1 can (19 oz) red kidney beans, drained, rinsed

1 can (6 oz) pitted large ripe olives, drained, cut in half

1 can (4.5 oz) chopped green chiles, drained

# mexican macaroni salad

**8 servings (1¼ cups each)** | Prep Time: **30 minutes** | Start to Finish: **1 hour 30 minutes**

1 Cook and drain pasta as directed on package. Rinse with cold water to cool; drain well.

2 Meanwhile, grate peel from limes; place in small bowl. Squeeze juice from limes; add to peel in bowl. Stir in dressing and taco seasoning mix. Stir avocado into dressing mixture.

3 In large serving bowl, toss pasta with all remaining ingredients. Pour dressing mixture over salad; toss gently to mix. Cover; refrigerate at least 1 hour before serving to blend flavors.

High Altitude **(3,500–6,500 ft): No change.**

**1 Serving:** Calories 560 (Calories from Fat 250); Total Fat 27g (Saturated Fat 7g; Trans Fat 0g); Cholesterol 75mg; Sodium 1210mg; Total Carbohydrate 61g (Dietary Fiber 8g; Sugars 4g); Protein 17g  **% Daily Value:** Vitamin A 15%; Vitamin C 30%; Calcium 15%; Iron 30%  **Exchanges:** 3½ Starch, ½ Other Carbohydrate, 1 Very Lean Meat, 5 Fat **Carbohydrate Choices:** 4

Cheryl Amato | South Amboy, NJ

**Cheryl Amato,** a computer consultant, put a Mexican twist on macaroni salad, an American favorite. She said this recipe is perfect for entertaining because it can be made ahead, which allows plenty of time to enjoy the party and the weekend. The salad has even been a side dish for the annual family pig roast.

6 taco shells (from 4.6-oz box), crushed to ½-inch pieces (about 1¼ cups)

2 cups frozen gold and white super sweet corn (from 1-lb bag)

1½ cups shredded Mexican 4-cheese blend (6 oz)

2 tablespoons chopped fresh cilantro

2 tablespoons chopped green onions (2 medium)

1 boneless pork loin roast (about 4 lb), trimmed of fat, butterflied by butcher to be flattened and rolled*

Salt and freshly cracked pepper, if desired

1 package (1.25 oz) taco seasoning mix

½ teaspoon garlic salt

½ teaspoon ground cumin

½ cup chicken broth

1½ teaspoons grated lime peel

1 tablespoon fresh lime juice

½ cup grape tomatoes or cherry tomatoes, cut in half

1 ripe avocado, pitted, peeled and cut into bite-size pieces

Lime slices, if desired

Additional fresh cilantro, if desired

*To cut pork roast so it can be filled and rolled, cut horizontally down length of pork, about ½ inch from top of pork, to within ½ inch of opposite side; open flat. Turn pork so you can cut other side. Repeat with other side of pork, cutting from the inside edge to within ½ inch of outer edge; open flat. Sprinkle with salt and pepper. Fill and roll as directed above.

Mary Edwards | Long Beach, CA

When **Mary Edwards** was 10, her mother spent six weeks in the hospital and taught her—via telephone—how to cook. She started with beans and franks and then advanced to meatloaf and mashed potatoes by the time her mother returned home. "Although I was the baby of the family, I could cook!" And cook she does. While living in Mexico, Mary prepared exotic fare like iguana and goat.

# piñata pork roast

**12 servings**  |  Prep Time: **30 minutes**  |  Start to Finish: **2 hours 10 minutes**

1  Heat oven to 350°F. In medium bowl, mix crushed taco shells, 1 cup of the frozen corn, the cheese, chopped cilantro and onions.

2  Open pork roast to lay flat; sprinkle with salt and pepper. Press taco shell mixture evenly onto pork to within about ¾ inch of edge.

3  Starting with one long side, tightly roll up pork jelly-roll fashion; tie with kitchen string at 1½-inch intervals. Rub taco seasoning mix evenly over rolled pork. Place seam side down on rack in ungreased large heavy ovenproof roasting pan. Insert ovenproof meat thermometer so tip is in center of thickest part of pork.

4  Roast uncovered 1 hour 15 minutes to 1 hour 30 minutes or until meat thermometer inserted into center of pork reads 155°F. Remove pork from pan; place on cutting board or serving platter. Cover with foil; let stand 10 minutes until thermometer reads 160°F.

5  If necessary, drain off any excess fat from roasting pan; place pan over medium-high heat. Stir in garlic salt, cumin, broth and remaining 1 cup corn. Cook 2 to 3 minutes, stirring occasionally, just until corn is tender. Stir in lime peel, lime juice, tomatoes and avocado. Cook just until thoroughly heated. Remove string from pork; cut across grain into slices. Serve pork with corn-avocado salsa; garnish with lime and cilantro.

High Altitude (3,500–6,500 ft): No change.

1 Serving: Calories 380 (Calories from Fat 180); Total Fat 20g (Saturated Fat 7g; Trans Fat 0.5g); Cholesterol 110mg; Sodium 530mg; Total Carbohydrate 12g (Dietary Fiber 2g; Sugars 1g); Protein 38g  % Daily Value: Vitamin A 8%; Vitamin C 4%; Calcium 10%; Iron 10%  Exchanges: 1 Starch, 5 Very Lean Meat, 3 Fat  Carbohydrate Choices: 1

1 to 2 tablespoons extra-virgin olive oil

5 uncooked mild Italian pork sausage links (about 1½ lb)

½ cup finely chopped onion (1 medium)

½ cup finely chopped carrot

1 clove garlic, finely chopped

½ cup finely chopped zucchini

2 tablespoons finely chopped fresh parsley

½ teaspoon dried basil leaves

½ teaspoon salt

¼ teaspoon pepper

1 can (28 oz) Italian-style peeled whole tomatoes (with basil), undrained, cut up

1 can (15 oz) cannellini (white kidney) beans, undrained

1 box (5.9 oz) Parmesan-flavor couscous mix

Butter

Water

2 tablespoons freshly grated Parmesan cheese

Judy Mortensen |
Citrus Heights, CA

According to **Judy Mortensen**, "If it goes horribly wrong, destroy all the evidence and deny everything." But this recipe, which originated when Judy began experimenting with new ways to cook tomatoes, is no mistake. It's easy to prepare, yet it tastes like more effort went into it.

# sausage ratatouille with couscous

**5 servings (1 sausage link, 1¼ cups beans, ½ cup couscous)** | Prep Time: **45 minutes** | Start to Finish: **45 minutes**

1 In 12-inch skillet, heat oil over medium heat. Add sausage links; cook and stir until browned on all sides. Remove from skillet; set aside. Add onion, carrot and garlic to skillet; cook and stir until onion becomes translucent. Stir in zucchini, parsley and basil. Cook 2 to 3 minutes, stirring occasionally. Stir in salt, pepper and tomatoes.

2 Return sausages to skillet. Heat to boiling. Reduce heat to medium-low; simmer uncovered 20 to 25 minutes, stirring occasionally, until liquid is reduced by half and meat thermometer inserted in center of sausages reads 160°F. Stir in beans. Cook until thoroughly heated.

3 Meanwhile, in 2-quart saucepan, make couscous with amounts of butter and water as directed on box.

4 To serve, fluff couscous; spoon around sides of large serving dish. Spoon tomato-vegetable mixture into center; arrange sausages over top. Sprinkle with Parmesan cheese.

High Altitude (3,500-6,500 ft): In step 1, cook over medium-high heat. In step 2, reduce heat to medium.

1 Serving: Calories 540 (Calories from Fat 210); Total Fat 24g (Saturated Fat 8g; Trans Fat 0g); Cholesterol 60mg; Sodium 1220mg; Total Carbohydrate 54g (Dietary Fiber 9g; Sugars 7g); Protein 27g % Daily Value: Vitamin A 40%; Vitamin C 15%; Calcium 20%; Iron 30% Exchanges: 3 Starch, ½ Other Carbohydrate, 2½ Medium-Fat Meat, 2 Fat Carbohydrate Choices: 3½

**Steak Rolls**

1 small papaya (about 1 lb), peeled,
  seeds removed

1 small box (1½ oz) raisins (about 4 heaping
  tablespoons)

3 teaspoons garlic powder

1 teaspoon salt

½ teaspoon pepper

4 thin (¼ to ⅛ inch thick) boneless beef
  top round steaks, cut by butcher (each
  6 to 8 oz, about 10 inches long and
  5 inches wide)

**Mojo Sauce**

12 pimiento-stuffed queen (large) Spanish
  olives, each cut into 4 slices, or ⅓ cup
  sliced green olives

1 small sweet onion, coarsely chopped
  (⅓ cup)

1 tablespoon drained capers

1 can (15 oz) black beans, undrained

1 can (28 oz) diced tomatoes, drained

---

Ava Peeples | Phoenix, AZ

**Ava Peeples**'s recipe blends flavors from her mother's beloved Puerto Rican dishes and Ava's favorite tastes from restaurant dishes. "To impress my mom, I tried to create a dish that would bring back good memories for her," said Ava. "But I couldn't resist the temptation to make a stuffed meat dish (like I learned from my German grandma) and put in extra garlic (like my Southern grandma)."

# papaya-raisin steak rolls in mojo sauce

**4 servings (1 steak roll and 1 cup mojo sauce each)** | Prep Time: **1 hour** | Start to Finish: **1 hour**

1 In small bowl, mash papaya with fork until fairly smooth but pulpy. Stir in raisins; set aside. In another small bowl, mix garlic powder, salt and pepper.

2 Place steaks side by side on waxed paper–lined work surface. Sprinkle garlic powder mixture evenly over one side of each steak; pat and press into steak. Turn steaks over; spread about 2 tablespoons papaya mixture in center of each steak. Starting with one short side, tightly roll up each steak; secure end with toothpick.

3 Spray 12-inch skillet (or 10-inch skillet, 2 inches deep) with cooking spray; heat skillet over medium heat. Add rolls to skillet; cook uncovered over medium heat 5 minutes. Turn rolls; cook 5 minutes longer. Meanwhile, in medium bowl, mix all mojo sauce ingredients.

4 Pour mojo sauce over steak rolls in skillet. Reduce heat to medium-low; simmer uncovered 20 to 30 minutes, stirring and spooning sauce over rolls occasionally, until meat thermometer inserted in center of rolls reads 140°F. Remove toothpicks; serve steak rolls topped with mojo sauce.

High Altitude (3,500–6,500 ft): In step 3, cook over medium-high heat. In step 4, cook over medium heat.

1 Serving: Calories 470 (Calories from Fat 80); Total Fat 8g (Saturated Fat 2.5g; Trans Fat 0g); Cholesterol 95mg; Sodium 1520mg; Total Carbohydrate 48g (Dietary Fiber 10g; Sugars 17g); Protein 50g  % Daily Value: Vitamin A 15%; Vitamin C 35%; Calcium 15%; Iron 45%  Exchanges: 2 Starch, 1 Other Carbohydrate, 1 Vegetable, 6 Very Lean Meat, ½ Fat  Carbohydrate Choices: 3

**Rolls**

2 cans (11 oz each) refrigerated French loaf

**Meatballs**

2 tablespoons extra-virgin olive oil

1 package (1.25 oz) taco seasoning mix

1 egg, slightly beaten

1 lb lean (at least 80%) ground beef

½ cup garlic-herb dry bread crumbs

½ cup chopped fresh cilantro

½ cup finely chopped onion (1 medium)

½ teaspoon finely chopped garlic

¼ teaspoon freshly ground black pepper

2 tablespoons chunky-style salsa

1 teaspoon red pepper sauce

**Sauce**

1¼ cups ranch dressing

¼ cup chopped fresh cilantro

¼ cup chunky-style salsa

1 tablespoon fresh lime juice

Reserved 1 teaspoon taco seasoning mix

**Toppings**

2 cups shredded iceberg lettuce

1 cup shredded Cheddar cheese (4 oz)

1 cup diced tomatoes (2 small)

¼ cup chopped fresh cilantro

---

Jenny Flake | Gilbert, AZ

**Jenny Flake** learned to cook after she got married. "I had no clue what I was doing!" she said. She does now. Her recipe jazzes up the traditional meatball sub by giving it a Mexican-style twist. Jenny's cooking has been influenced by her mother, her father-in-law and her French grandmother, the latter of whom "is all about taste—forget the calories!"

# toasted mexi-meatball hoagies

**4 servings (½ sandwich each)** | Prep Time: **45 minutes** | Start to Finish: **1 hour 15 minutes**

1  Heat oven to 350°F. Grease large cookie sheet with cooking spray or shortening. Remove dough from both cans; place seam side down and 3 inches apart on cookie sheet. Cut 4 or 5 diagonal slashes (½-inch deep) with sharp knife on top of each loaf. Bake 26 to 30 minutes or until deep golden brown. Cool slightly while preparing meatballs, about 25 minutes.

2  Spread oil in bottom of 13 × 9-inch (3-quart) glass baking dish. Reserve 1 teaspoon of the taco seasoning mix for sauce; place remaining seasoning mix in large bowl. Add remaining meatball ingredients; mix well. Shape mixture into 1-inch balls; place in baking dish. Bake uncovered 25 to 30 minutes, turning meatballs once halfway through baking, until meat thermometer inserted in center of meatballs reads 160°F.

3  Meanwhile, in food processor, place all sauce ingredients; process until smooth. Set aside.

4  Set oven control to broil. Cut each loaf in half horizontally, cutting to but not completely through one long side; place cut side up on cookie sheet. Broil 5 to 6 inches from heat 1 to 2 minutes or just until lightly toasted.

5  Spread ¼ cup sauce on each toasted cut side. Spoon hot meatballs evenly onto bottom halves of loaf. Top evenly with toppings. Drizzle with remaining sauce. If desired, close sandwiches. Cut each sandwich in half. Serve immediately.

High Altitude (3,500–6,500 ft): No change.

**1 Serving:** Calories 1240 (Calories from Fat 660); Total Fat 74g (Saturated Fat 20g; Trans Fat 2.5g); Cholesterol 175mg; Sodium 3000mg; Total Carbohydrate 98g (Dietary Fiber 5g; Sugars 14g); Protein 45g  **% Daily Value:** Vitamin A 30%; Vitamin C 30%; Calcium 25%; Iron 50%  **Exchanges:** 5 Starch, 1 Other Carbohydrate, 1 Vegetable, 4 Medium-Fat Meat, 10 Fat  **Carbohydrate Choices:** 6½

4 large boneless skinless chicken breasts
(5 to 6 oz each)*

2 cups crispy horn-shaped corn
snacks, crushed**

1 can (4.5 oz) chopped green chiles, drained

6 oz queso fresco (Mexican cheese), cut
into 4 equal slices

Salt and pepper, if desired

1 cup frozen whole kernel corn (from 1-lb
bag), thawed

1 tablespoon olive oil

⅓ cup roasted red bell peppers (4 oz
from jar)

1 cup whipping cream

½ cup water

2 tablespoons unsalted or regular butter
or margarine

2 teaspoons finely chopped fresh garlic

1 chicken bouillon cube

4 flour tortillas (10 to 12 inch)

2 cups cooked white rice

2 tablespoons chopped fresh cilantro

*Each chicken breast must weigh at
least 5 ounces for success of recipe.

**To crush corn snacks, place in
resealable food-storage plastic bag;
seal bag and crush with rolling pin.

Tori Johnson | Gilbert, AZ

Every year **Tori Johnson**
takes her restaurant's
employees on a camping
trip. They build boats out
of cardboard boxes and
race them. And, she said, "we eat like
kings." With Tori in the kitchen, so
does her family. She likes to cook
using vibrant colors and readily
available products. This chicken
dish looks like a festive, colorful
piece of art.

# baked sonoran chicken

**4 servings** | Prep Time: **1 hour** | Start to Finish: **1 hour**

1 Heat oven to 425°F. Line cookie sheet with foil. Place each chicken breast,
smooth side down, between pieces of plastic wrap or waxed paper; gently
pound with flat side of meat mallet or rolling pin until about ¼ inch thick.

2 Over each chicken breast, sprinkle ¼ cup crushed corn snacks and ¼ of the
green chiles; place 1 slice cheese in center. Fold ends of chicken over and
tuck in sides; secure with toothpicks. Sprinkle with salt and pepper. Place
seam side down on one side of cookie sheet. In small bowl, toss thawed corn
with oil. Place corn on other side of cookie sheet. Bake 20 minutes.

3 Meanwhile, in blender, place roasted peppers, whipping cream and water;
cover and blend on high speed 15 seconds or until smooth. In 2-quart
saucepan, melt butter over medium heat. Add garlic; cook and stir 1
minute. Add pepper mixture and bouillon cube; heat to boiling. Cook,
stirring constantly, until sauce is reduced and thickened, about 15 minutes.

4 Remove chicken from cookie sheet; place on cutting board. Let stand
5 minutes. Cut chicken into ¼-inch-thick slices.

5 In 12-inch skillet, heat each tortilla over high heat until blistered on each
side; place on individual dinner plates. Place ½ cup rice on one half of
each tortilla; fan slices of 1 chicken breast leaning on rice. Top chicken on
each evenly with roasted pepper sauce, roasted corn and cilantro.

High Altitude (3,500–6,500 ft): No change.

1 **Serving:** Calories 910 (Calories from Fat 400); Total Fat 45g (Saturated Fat 24g; Trans Fat 2g); Cholesterol 180mg;
Sodium 1300mg; Total Carbohydrate 80g (Dietary Fiber 3g; Sugars 5g); Protein 48g **% Daily Value:** Vitamin A 40%;
Vitamin C 30%; Calcium 30%; Iron 30% **Exchanges:** 5 Starch, 4½ Very Lean Meat, 8 Fat **Carbohydrate Choices:** 5

**Crust**

1 refrigerated pie crust (from 15-oz box),
softened as directed on box

**Fudge Layer and Drizzle**

1¼ cups dark or semisweet chocolate chips
(7½ oz)

½ cup whipping cream

2 tablespoons butter

**Filling**

1¼ cups milk

1 container (6 oz) French vanilla
low-fat yogurt

1 box (4-serving size) white chocolate
instant pudding and pie filling mix

3 tablespoons butter

1 bag (10 oz) peanut butter chips (1⅔ cups)

**Topping**

4 peanut butter crunchy granola bars
(2 pouches from 8.9-oz box), crushed
(¾ cup)*

*To easily crush granola bars, do not
unwrap; use rolling pin to crush bars.

Claudia Shepardson |
South Yarmouth, MA

**Claudia Shepardson**
created this pie on the day
before the Bake-Off®
deadline, then served it
to her family after her
grandson's Little League game. One
morning she felt strongly that she
would get a notification call that
day. When Caller ID showed a call
from Minnesota, the home of the
Bake-Off® Contest team, Claudia
said she was "already pretty much in
a state of shock."

# black-bottom peanut butter pie

**8 servings** | Prep Time: **25 minutes** | Start to Finish: **3 hours 25 minutes**

1 Heat oven to 450°F. Make pie crust as directed on box for One-Crust
Baked Shell using 9-inch glass pie plate. Cool on wire rack 20 minutes.

2 Meanwhile, in 1-quart heavy saucepan, mix all fudge layer ingredients.
Cook over low heat, stirring constantly, until chips are melted. Remove
from heat; stir until smooth. Reserve ¼ cup fudge mixture in small
microwavable bowl for drizzle; set remaining mixture aside to cool.

3 In large bowl, beat milk, yogurt and pudding mix with electric mixer on
high speed about 3 minutes or until smooth and thickened. Set aside.

4 In another small microwavable bowl, microwave 3 tablespoons butter and
the peanut butter chips on High 45 seconds. Stir; if necessary, continue
to microwave in 10-second increments, stirring after each, until chips are
melted and mixture is smooth. On low speed, gradually beat peanut butter
mixture into pudding mixture until combined; beat on high speed until
filling is smooth and fluffy, scraping side of bowl occasionally.

5 Spread cooled fudge layer mixture evenly in bottom of cooled baked shell.
Carefully spoon and spread filling over fudge layer. Sprinkle crushed
granola bars evenly over top. Refrigerate until set, 3 to 4 hours.

6 To serve, microwave reserved fudge mixture on High 15 to 20 seconds or
until drizzling consistency. Drizzle over top of pie. Cut into wedges to
serve. Store in refrigerator.

High Altitude (3,500–6,500 ft): No change.

1 Serving: Calories 690 (Calories from Fat 360); Total Fat 40g (Saturated Fat 18g; Trans Fat 0.5g); Cholesterol 45mg;
Sodium 520mg; Total Carbohydrate 72g (Dietary Fiber 3g; Sugars 48g); Protein 10g  % Daily Value: Vitamin A 10%;
Vitamin C 0%; Calcium 10%; Iron 8% Exchanges: 2 Starch, 3 Other Carbohydrate, ½ High-Fat Meat, 7 Fat **Carbohydrate
Choices: 5**

## Crust

12 pecan shortbread cookies, broken into pieces

4 pecan crunch crunchy granola bars (2 pouches from 8.9-oz box), crushed (¾ cup)*

⅓ cup butter, melted

## Chocolate Filling

2 oz cream cheese (from 8-oz package), softened

¼ cup powdered sugar

1 tablespoon milk

¼ cup semisweet chocolate chips, melted, cooled

1 container (8 oz) frozen (thawed) whipped topping

## Coconut-Pecan Filling

1 container (15 oz) coconut-pecan creamy ready-to-spread frosting

2 oz cream cheese (from 8-oz package), softened

1 tablespoon milk

1 container (8 oz) frozen (thawed) whipped topping

## Garnishes

Reserved ½ cup whipped topping

½ milk chocolate candy bar (1.55-oz size) or ½ dark chocolate candy bar (1.44-oz size), unwrapped, chopped

*To easily crush granola bars, do not unwrap; use rolling pin to crush bars.

Annette Mease | Boise, ID

**Annette Mease,** who loves the flavor of German chocolate, adapted her creation from a recipe for chocolate–peanut butter pie. She started experimenting and "changed everything." Annette describes this pie as a no-bake recipe that melts in your mouth, creamy and light, with just the right blend of flavors. Her family loves it.

# german chocolate cream pie

**8 servings** | Prep Time: **1 hour** | Start to Finish: **2 hours 30 minutes**

1 In food processor or blender, process cookies and granola bars with on-and-off motions until fine crumbs form; pour into medium bowl. Stir in melted butter with fork until well mixed. Press mixture in bottom and up side of ungreased 9- or 8-inch glass or metal pie plate. Place in freezer just until firm, about 10 minutes.

2 Meanwhile, in medium bowl, beat 2 oz cream cheese, the powdered sugar and 1 tablespoon milk with electric mixer on medium speed until blended. On low speed, beat in melted chocolate chips. In small bowl, reserve ¼ cup whipped topping from 8-oz container for garnish. On medium speed, beat remaining topping from container into chocolate mixture until well blended.

3 Spread ⅓ cup of the frosting evenly in bottom of crust. Spoon chocolate filling into crust; carefully spread. Place pie in freezer while making next layer.

4 In large bowl, beat 2 oz cream cheese, 1 tablespoon milk and remaining frosting with electric mixer on medium speed until well blended. Reserve another ¼ cup whipped topping from 8-oz container in same small bowl of topping. Beat remaining topping from container into coconut-pecan mixture until well blended. Carefully spoon over chocolate filling; spread evenly. Carefully spread reserved ½ cup whipped topping over top; sprinkle with chopped candy bar. Refrigerate 1 hour 30 minutes before serving.

High Altitude (3,500–6,500 ft): No change.

1 Serving: Calories 770 (Calories from Fat 470); Total Fat 53g (Saturated Fat 31g; Trans Fat 2g); Cholesterol 90mg; Sodium 260mg; Total Carbohydrate 67g (Dietary Fiber 4g; Sugars 47g); Protein 8g  **% Daily Value:** Vitamin A 10%; Vitamin C 0%; Calcium 10%; Iron 8%  **Exchanges:** 1½ Starch, 3 Other Carbohydrate, ½ High-Fat Meat, 9 Fat **Carbohydrate Choices:** 4½

1 box (19.5 oz) fudge brownie mix

½ cup vegetable oil

¼ cup water

4 eggs

1 cup semisweet chocolate chips (6 oz)

2 packages (8 oz each) cream cheese, softened

½ cup sugar

1 container (6 oz) vanilla thick & creamy low-fat yogurt

1 can (21 oz) cherry pie filling

1 aerosol can whipped cream topping

1 large sprig fresh mint, if desired

Kyle O'Malley |
Brigantine Beach, NJ

"My husband loves chocolate and cheesecake," said **Kyle O'Malley**. "I combined the two and added the cherries because I love them." Her resulting dessert recipe is not only simple and fun, it "packs that 'wow' factor when you present it." Kyle was instilled with a love of cooking from her mother and grandmother. "I know my grandmother would be proud."

# black forest cheesecake dessert cups

**24 dessert cups**  |  Prep Time: **55 minutes**  |  Start to Finish: **2 hours 50 minutes**

1 Heat oven to 350°F. Place paper baking cup in each of 24 large muffin cups (2¾ inches in diameter and 1¼ inches deep). Make brownie mix as directed on box using oil, water and 2 of the eggs. Divide batter evenly among muffin cups (about 2 tablespoons per cup). Bake 15 minutes.

2 Meanwhile, in small microwavable bowl, microwave chocolate chips on High 1 minute. Stir and microwave in 15-second increments, stirring after each, until chips are melted and smooth; set aside. In large bowl, beat cream cheese with electric mixer on medium speed until smooth. Beat in sugar, remaining 2 eggs and the yogurt until blended. Add melted chocolate; beat until well blended.

3 Divide chocolate mixture evenly over warm brownie layer in cups (about 3 tablespoons per cup), filling each to top of cup. Cups will be full.

4 Bake 22 to 26 minutes longer or until set. Cool in pans 20 to 30 minutes. Carefully remove dessert cups from pan (cream cheese mixture will be soft); place on serving platter. Refrigerate at least 1 hour before serving.

5 To serve, remove paper; top each dessert cup with 1 tablespoon pie filling (including 2 or 3 cherries) and 1 tablespoon whipped cream topping. If desired, arrange cupcakes on pedestal cake plate covered with linen napkin. Garnish platter or plate with mint sprig. Store in refrigerator.

High Altitude (3,500–6,500 ft): Stir ½ cup flour into dry brownie mix. Increase water to ⅓ cup. Makes 30 dessert cups.

**1 Dessert Cup:** Calories 330 (Calories from Fat 160); Total Fat 18g (Saturated Fat 8g; Trans Fat 0g); Cholesterol 65mg; Sodium 150mg; Total Carbohydrate 36g (Dietary Fiber 2g; Sugars 29g); Protein 4g  % **Daily Value:** Vitamin A 8%; Vitamin C 0%; Calcium 4%; Iron 8%  **Exchanges:** 1 Starch, 1½ Other Carbohydrate, 3½ Fat  **Carbohydrate Choices:** 2½

## Crust

2 cups Golden Grahams® cereal, finely crushed (¾ cup)

6 pecan crunch crunchy granola bars (3 pouches from 8.9-oz box), finely crushed (heaping 1 cup)*

½ cup chopped pecans, ground

2 tablespoons sugar

7 tablespoons butter or margarine, melted

## Filling

¼ cup Key lime or regular lime juice

½ package (1½ teaspoons) unflavored gelatin

1 package (8 oz) cream cheese, softened

1 box (4-serving size) lemon instant pudding and pie filling mix

3 containers (6 oz each) Key lime pie low-fat yogurt

½ cup sugar

½ cup chopped pecans

*To easily crush granola bars, do not unwrap; use rolling pin to crush bars.

Sue Tyner | Tustin, CA

When she's not helping people or pets, you'll find **Sue Tyner** in her kitchen, happily experimenting. She keeps a laptop on her kitchen counter to capture each version of her recipes as they evolve. Sue said this tart "is easy to prepare and tastes out of this world." She gets many of her ideas in the grocery store. "There are so many more products available today, the possibilities are endless."

# key lime–pecan tart

**12 servings** | Prep Time: **25 minutes** | Start to Finish: **2 hours 35 minutes**

1 Heat oven to 350°F. In medium bowl, mix all crust ingredients. Press in bottom and up side of ungreased 11- or 10-inch tart pan with removable bottom. Bake 10 minutes. Cool 10 minutes. Place in freezer while making filling.

2 Meanwhile, in 1-cup microwavable measuring cup or small bowl, place lime juice. Stir in gelatin. Microwave on High about 30 seconds, stirring occasionally, until gelatin is dissolved; set aside.

3 In large bowl, beat cream cheese with electric mixer on medium speed until light and fluffy. Add gelatin mixture and pudding mix; beat until smooth, scraping bowl frequently. Add 1 container of yogurt at a time, beating well after each addition. Gradually beat in ½ cup sugar until smooth.

4 Spread filling evenly in crust; sprinkle with pecans. Refrigerate at least 2 hours before serving. Cut into wedges to serve. Store in refrigerator.

High Altitude (3,500–6,500 ft): No change.

1 **Serving:** Calories 380 (Calories from Fat 200); Total Fat 22g (Saturated Fat 9g; Trans Fat 0.5g); Cholesterol 40mg; Sodium 350mg; Total Carbohydrate 41g (Dietary Fiber 2g; Sugars 30g); Protein 6g  **% Daily Value:** Vitamin A 15%; Vitamin C 2%; Calcium 10%; Iron 10%  **Exchanges:** ½ Starch, 2 Other Carbohydrate, ½ High-Fat Meat, 3½ Fat **Carbohydrate Choices:** 3

1 roll (16.5 oz) refrigerated sugar cookies

1 bag (12 oz) white vanilla baking chips (2 cups)

1 cup organic frozen raspberries (from 10-oz bag), thawed

1 container (16 oz) lemon creamy ready-to-spread frosting

1 package (8 oz) cream cheese, softened

1 teaspoon lemon extract

1 container (8 oz) frozen (thawed) whipped topping

1 teaspoon vegetable oil, if desired

Kathryn Friedl | Lawton, OK

**Kathryn Friedl** is proud to be a Bake-Off® finalist. "Everyone thought it was so silly to enter," said Kathryn. "Who's silly now?" She loves quick and tasty desserts and created this treat specifically for the contest. The best cooking advice Kathryn ever received was, "Don't be afraid to experiment."

# fluffy lemon-raspberry treat

**24 servings**  |  Prep Time: **20 minutes**  |  Start to Finish: **2 hours 25 minutes**

1  Heat oven to 350°F. Grease 13 × 9-inch pan with shortening. Break up cookie dough into pan; press in bottom to form crust. Bake 13 to 18 minutes or until golden brown. Immediately sprinkle 1 cup of the white chips evenly over cookie crust. Let stand 5 minutes. Spread evenly with back of spoon. Cool completely, about 30 minutes.

2  Meanwhile, in small bowl, stir ½ cup of the raspberries with fork until broken up and slightly mashed. Refrigerate. In large bowl, beat frosting, cream cheese and lemon extract with electric mixer on medium-high speed about 2 minutes or until well blended. Fold in whipped topping. Refrigerate.

3  Spread mashed raspberries over cooled crust. Place in freezer for 15 minutes. Spread frosting mixture over raspberries. Refrigerate until set, about 1 hour.

4  To serve, in small bowl, mash remaining ½ cup raspberries with fork. Spread raspberries over frosting mixture. In small resealable freezer plastic bag, place remaining 1 cup white chips and the oil; seal bag. Microwave on High 1 minute. Squeeze bag to mix; microwave in 10-second increments, squeezing after each, until chips are melted and smooth. Cut small hole in one bottom corner of bag; squeeze bag to drizzle mixture over top of dessert. Cut into squares to serve. Store in refrigerator.

High Altitude (3,500–6,500 ft): Break up cookie dough into bowl. Knead or stir 3 tablespoons flour into cookie dough before pressing into bottom of pan.

1 Serving: Calories 310 (Calories from Fat 140); Total Fat 16g (Saturated Fat 10g; Trans Fat 1g); Cholesterol 20mg; Sodium 115mg; Total Carbohydrate 39g (Dietary Fiber 1g; Sugars 31g); Protein 3g  **% Daily Value:** Vitamin A 2%; Vitamin C 2%; Calcium 4%; Iron 4%  **Exchanges:** 1 Starch, 1½ Other Carbohydrate, 3 Fat  **Carbohydrate Choices:** 2½

**Brownie Layers**

1 box (19.5 oz) fudge brownie mix

½ cup vegetable oil

¼ cup water

3 eggs

**Strawberry Cream**

3 tablespoons granulated sugar

1 package (8 oz) cream cheese, softened

1 container (6 oz) strawberry thick & creamy
low-fat yogurt

1½ cups finely chopped fresh strawberries

**Chocolate Fudge**

½ cup whipping cream

1½ cups semisweet chocolate chips (9 oz)

**Garnish**

6 small to medium fresh whole
strawberries, halved

1 teaspoon powdered sugar

Rebecca Kremer  |  Hudson, WI

**Rebecca Kremer's** inspiration for her torte recipe came from the beautiful, multi-layered cakes seen in fine bakeries. "I wanted to make something equally beautiful, but easy," she said. Her torte looks quite elaborate, yet requires just five steps. Rebecca served the torte in celebration of her in-laws' 60th wedding anniversary. Her father-in-law said, "This could be a winner," and ate two pieces.

# fudge-strawberry cream torte

**12 servings**  |  Prep Time: **1 hour 15 minutes**  |  Start to Finish: **3 hours 10 minutes**

1  Heat oven to 350°F. Spray bottoms of 2 (9-inch) round cake pans with cooking spray.\* Make brownie mix as directed on box for cake-like brownies using oil, water and eggs. Spread half of batter evenly in each pan. Bake 18 to 23 minutes. Cool on wire racks 10 minutes. Run knife around brownie layers to loosen. Place wire racks upside down over pans; turn racks and pans over. Remove pans. Cool completely, about 35 minutes.

2  Meanwhile, in small bowl, beat granulated sugar and cream cheese with electric mixer on medium speed until well blended. Beat in strawberry yogurt until smooth and creamy. Fold in chopped strawberries. Refrigerate while brownie layers cool.

3  In 1-quart saucepan, heat whipping cream over medium heat, stirring constantly, just until cream begins to boil. Remove from heat. Add chocolate chips; press into cream. Cover; let stand 3 minutes. Vigorously beat with wire whisk until smooth. Cool completely, about 30 minutes.

4  To assemble torte, place 1 brownie layer on serving plate. Spread half of strawberry cream evenly over brownie to within 1 inch of edge. Carefully spoon and spread half of chocolate fudge almost to edge of strawberry cream. Repeat layers, ending with chocolate fudge. Arrange halved strawberries in spoke fashion on top of torte. Refrigerate at least 1 hour before serving.

5  To serve,\*\* sprinkle powdered sugar over top of torte and around plate. Carefully cut torte with hot knife into wedges to avoid "cracking" of chocolate fudge on top. Store loosely covered in refrigerator.

High Altitude (3,500–6,500 ft): Stir ½ cup flour into dry brownie mix. Increase water to ⅓ cup. Bake 21 to 25 minutes.

1 **Serving:** Calories 550 (Calories from Fat 280); Total Fat 31g (Saturated Fat 13g; Trans Fat 0g); Cholesterol 85mg; Sodium 210mg; Total Carbohydrate 61g (Dietary Fiber 3g; Sugars 45g); Protein 7g  **% Daily Value:** Vitamin A 10%; Vitamin C 25%; Calcium 6%; Iron 15%  **Exchanges:** 1 Starch, 3 Other Carbohydrate, ½ High-Fat Meat, 5 Fat  **Carbohydrate Choices:** 4

\*For easy pan removal, line bottoms of pans with waxed paper before spraying with cooking spray.

\*\*If torte has been stored for more than 3 hours before serving, let stand at room temperature 10 minutes before cutting.

# metric conversion guide

## VOLUME

| U.S. Units | Canadian Metric | Australian Metric |
|---|---|---|
| ¼ teaspoon | 1 mL | 1 ml |
| ½ teaspoon | 2 mL | 2 ml |
| 1 teaspoon | 5 mL | 5 ml |
| 1 tablespoon | 15 mL | 20 ml |
| ¼ cup | 50 mL | 60 ml |
| ⅓ cup | 75 mL | 80 ml |
| ½ cup | 125 mL | 125 ml |
| ⅔ cup | 150 mL | 170 ml |
| ¾ cup | 175 mL | 190 ml |
| 1 cup | 250 mL | 250 ml |
| 1 quart | 1 liter | 1 liter |
| 1½ quarts | 1.5 liters | 1.5 liters |
| 2 quarts | 2 liters | 2 liters |
| 2½ quarts | 2.5 liters | 2.5 liters |
| 3 quarts | 3 liters | 3 liters |
| 4 quarts | 4 liters | 4 liters |

## WEIGHT

| U.S. Units | Canadian Metric | Australian Metric |
|---|---|---|
| 1 ounce | 30 grams | 30 grams |
| 2 ounces | 55 grams | 60 grams |
| 3 ounces | 85 grams | 90 grams |
| 4 ounces (¼ pound) | 115 grams | 125 grams |
| 8 ounces (½ pound) | 225 grams | 225 grams |
| 16 ounces (1 pound) | 455 grams | 500 grams |
| 1 pound | 455 grams | ½ kilogram |

Note: The recipes in this cookbook have not been developed or tested using metric measures. When converting recipes to metric, some variations in quality may be noted.

## MEASUREMENTS

| Inches | Centimeters |
|---|---|
| 1 | 2.5 |
| 2 | 5.0 |
| 3 | 7.5 |
| 4 | 10.0 |
| 5 | 12.5 |
| 6 | 15.0 |
| 7 | 17.5 |
| 8 | 20.5 |
| 9 | 23.0 |
| 10 | 25.5 |
| 11 | 28.0 |
| 12 | 30.5 |
| 13 | 33.0 |

## TEMPERATURES

| Fahrenheit | Celsius |
|---|---|
| 32° | 0° |
| 212° | 100° |
| 250° | 120° |
| 275° | 140° |
| 300° | 150° |
| 325° | 160° |
| 350° | 180° |
| 375° | 190° |
| 400° | 200° |
| 425° | 220° |
| 450° | 230° |
| 475° | 240° |
| 500° | 260° |

# index

## RECIPES

# CONTESTANTS